USAF Jet Powered Fighters

XP-59 - XF-85

Hugh Harkins

USAF Jet Powered Fighters - XP-59 - XF-85

© Hugh Harkins 2013

Published by Centurion Publishing
United Kingdom
G65 9YE

ISBN 13: 978-1-903630-31-0
ISBN 10: 1-903630-31-2

This volume first published in 2013

The Author is identified as the copyright holder of this work under sections 77 and 78 of the Copyright Designs and Patents Act 1988

Cover design © Centurion Publishing & Createspace

Page layout, concept and design © Centurion Publishing

All rights reserved. No part of this publication may be reproduced, stored in a retrieval system, transmitted in any form, or by any means, electronic, mechanical or photocopied, recorded or otherwise, without the written permission of the Publishers

The Publishers and Author would like to thank all companies and services for their assistance and contributions in the preparation of this publication

Contents

Introduction	3
Bell P-59 Airacomet	5
Northrop XP-79 Flying Ram	14
Lockheed F-80 Shooting Star	18
Consolidated Vultee (Convair) XP-81	40
Bell XP-83	44
Republic F-84 Thunderjet	47
Republic F-84F Thunderstreak	72
McDonnell XF-85 Goblin	88
Glossary	96

Introduction

Today recognised as a World leader in aircraft design and manufacture, the United States entered World War II trailing years behind its European rivals in the then new field of jet turbine propulsion. Its fledgling jet fighter programs took their tentative first steps in the early 1940's with the assistance of British jet turbine technology, allowing the United States to become the fourth nation to fly a turbojet-powered aircraft when the Bell XP-59 Airacomet took to the air on 1 October 1942. Germany and Britain had previously flown jet-powered aircraft in 1939 and 1941 respectively. The German Heinkel He 178 was the first aircraft in the world to fly under turbojet power when it took to the air on 27 August 1939. The first British jet powered aircraft to fly was the Gloster E.28/39, which conducted its maiden flight on 15 May 1941 under the power of a Whittle W.1 gas turbine. Italy flew the Caproni Campini N.1 experimental aircraft on 27 August 1940 and although there are some doubts over its credibility as a true jet powered aircraft, it is listed as such here. The aircraft, however, was nothing more than an experimental design with no potential for development as an operational aircraft. Its performance was very limited in comparison to conventional aircraft of the time.

In the United States Major General Harry Hap Arnold, Chief of the US Army Air Corp, on 25 February 1941 sent a letter to Chairman of NACA (National Advisory Committee for Aeronautics), Dr Vannevar Bush requesting that he "form a special group" whose purpose was to consider possible applications of jet turbine propulsion. The following month Bush formed the "Special Committee on Jet Propulsion", which included personnel from the Army Air Corp, Navy Bureau of Aeronautics, National Bureau of Standards, Johns Hopkins University, Massachusetts Institute of Technology and Allis Chalmers, Westinghouse and General Electric. These last three companies were the three principal developers and manufactures of Industrial Turbines and turbine Superchargers in the US.

In summer 1941, a United States government and military delegation of three was in the United Kingdom and were taken on a tour of the Gloster factory on 28 July, at which time a formal request by the United States government was issued for specifications and drawings of both the Gloster E.28/39 and F.9/40 experimental jet aircraft. Within 11 days the British government had agreed to the requests, which effectively launched the American jet fighter program. The British governments willingness to supply what were closely guarded secrets stemmed from Prime Minister Churchill's desire to appease the US government, firstly to ensure the supply of lend-lease materials and secondly in the hope that the US would join in the Allied war effort against the Axis powers of Italy and Germany.

As well as the aircraft technical details, complete drawings of the Whittle W.2B and the actual W.1X non-flight rated engine were sent to the US in autumn 1941. A variant of the W.1, designated Type I-A, was built by General Electric, with assistance from Frank Whittle, who had travelled from Britain to the United States, and this was used to power the Bell XP-59, America's first jet powered aircraft, which conducted its first flight on 1 October 1942.

Often air brushed from history is the fact that Major General Arnold was informed of British progress in jet engine development as early as September 1940. Arnold was reported as being "shocked" by the progress of Britain, which combined with reports that Germany was also working on this revolutionary new power application, resulted in him ordering an enquiry into why the United States was so far behind. Arnold was apparently also present for the Gloster E.28/39's early taxi trials and "was absolutely stunned by how far the British had advanced." It would later be accepted in official documents that the United States lagging so far behind Great Britain and Germany in regards to jet propulsion was the "most serious inferiority in American aeronautical development which appeared during the Second World War."

Many of the early US jet powered aircraft were powered by turbojets based on British designs. However, the United States unique economic rise during and following the end of World War II, combined with the destruction in Europe and the post war financial burden of post war re-construction placed on Great Britain saw the US aircraft industry dominate the western combat and civil aircraft market in the decades following the end of the war.

This volume covers every turbojet powered fighter aircraft to enter service or be developed for the United States Air Force and its forebear the United States Army Air Force, from the XP-59, which flew in 1942, to the XF-85 which flew in 1948. While no US designed jet aircraft saw operational service during World War II, many would be employed in the 1950 – 1953 Korean War, including the Lockheed F-80 and Republic F-84, both of which were employed in large numbers.

Bell P-59 Airacomet

The Bell P-59, the first US built turbojet aircraft, was designed to provide the USAAF with a jet fighter during World War II. This XP-59A is seen at Muroc Dry Lake in the early 1940's. USAF

Prior to its entry into WW II the United States was years behind Britain and Germany in development of jet engine technology. Under technology transfer agreements the UK provided the US with technical data and complete engines developed from the work undertaken by Frank Whittle, the pioneer of Britain's first jet turbine engines. In addition, the US received complete plans for jet powered aircraft being developed in Britain including the Gloster E.28/39 and the F.9/40, which was developed into the Meteor, which entered RAF service in July 1944. Access to British jet engine technology would prove essential to the fledgling USAAF jet aircraft program.

The Bell P-59 Airacomet was designed as the USAAF, progenitor of the USAF, first jet powered combat aircraft. General H..H. Arnold ordered the commencement of development of what would become the P-59 on 4 September 1941. Initially the XP-59 was designed as a pusher propeller driven fighter designed from the XP-52. With the US being left behind by the developments in jet powered aircraft in Europe, particularly Germany and the United Kingdom, the USAAF wanted to get a jet fighter into development and eventually into operational service.

Initially the XP-59 was designed as a pusher-propeller design before the US gained access to British jet technology. This wind-tunnel model of the XP-59A shows the twin-boom configuration initially planned. USAFM

5

An XP-59A sits on the ramp at Muroc in 1942. The XP-59A's were painted in army olive drab, which was used on a number of aircraft at the time. AFFTC

Britain flew the Gloster E.28/39, its first experimental jet powered aircraft, on 15 May 1941. Within weeks a US government and military delegation of three was in the UK and were taken on a tour of the Gloster factory on 28 July 1941, at which time a formal request by the US was issued for specifications and drawings of both the Gloster E.28/39 and the Gloster F.9/40 (which became the Gloster Meteor), Britain's first operational jet fighter aircraft). Within 11 days, the British government had agreed to the requests, which effectively launched the United States jet fighter program, which without access to British data and hardware, would have been left more-or-less dead in the water. The British governments willingness to supply what were closely guarded secrets stemmed from Prime Minister Churchill's desire to appease the US government, firstly to ensure the supply of lend-lease materials and secondly in the hope that the United States would soon join in the Allied war effort against the Axis powers of Italy and Germany. In the event, the US refrained from joining in the war effort against Germany even after the Japanese attack on Pearl Harbour on 7 December 1941, and only found herself at war with Germany after Germany declared war on the US on 11 December 1941..

With access to British jet technology making a jet powered fighter aircraft for the USAAF a real possibility in the short-term, the pusher propeller concept originally planned for the XP-59 was abandoned in favour of jet turbine power. General Electric in the US took on the job of building the jet engines developed from the British W.1 and W.2 jet engines and Bell Aircraft was selected to build the airframe, which emerged as a mid-set straight wing

Top: Three XP-59A prototypes were ordered with the first aircraft completed around mid-1942. Above: This XP-59A on Muroc Dry Lake bed has been fitted with a dummy propeller in an effort to disguise the aircrafts jet power. Both USAF

design, which like the early German and British experimental jets held little promise of any great leap in capability over existing piston engine fighter aircraft.

Initially the XP-59 concept featured a twin-boom tail, but this was dropped in favour of a single-vertical tail before production of the prototype commenced. Production P-59's had a shorter vertical tail than the prototypes and the vertical stabiliser and wingtips were squared compared with the rounded stabiliser and wingtips of the X and YP-59's. The YP-59A had nose armament installed, allowing them to be easily distinguishable from the XP-59's.

Initially the XP-59 concept featured main undercarriage units located under the wings, outboard of the engines, which were positioned below the wings, one on each side of the fuselage. The main undercarriage gear retracted inwards to be housed in the wing, while the nose-wheel unit retracted aft to lie in the forward fuselage. The P-59 could be fitted with a pair of external drop fuel tanks of a standard type found on many USAAF fighter aircraft.

Top: The first XP-59 took to the air for the first time from Muroc Dry Lake on 1 October 1942. Above: The YP-59A differed from the XP-59A's in having a nose mounted gun armament. USAF

The project was shrouded in a veil of secrecy, with production of the prototype being conducted at Bell Aircraft. The low thrust ratings of early jet engines dictated that the P-59 would have to be powered by two-engines as were the first production British and German jet fighters; the Gloster Meteor and Messerschmitt Me.262 respectively. The P-59 was to be powered by a pair of General Electric I-A, 1-14 and finally I-16 turbojets based on the British Whittle jet engines; the I-16 producing only 1,650-lb's of thrust in the definitive P-59B, which was the main production variant.

The production standard P-59B was powered by two General Electric built I-16 turbojets rated at 1,650-lb thrust each. With these engines fitted the aircraft was capable of speeds of just over 400-mph. USAF

Three jet powered XP-59A prototypes were ordered with construction of the first aircraft being completed in mid-1942. Powered by two General Electric I-A turbojet engines, the first XP-59A conducted its maiden flight at Muroc Dry Lake (now Edwards AFB), California on 1 October 1942, bringing the US into the jet era, but still trailing some way behind Britain and Germany, particularly since the US program was largely reliant on British technical assistance.

In 1943 the P-59A was ordered into production powered by a pair of I-14 turbojets, which was an improved variant of the I-A. Thirteen YP-59A's and 20 P-59A production aircraft followed the three XP-59A prototypes. The YP-59A's, most of which were delivered during 1944, were used as service test aircraft to gain experience for the introduction of the P-59A and became the first production jet powered aircraft to enter service with the USAAF. The only other variant was the P-59B, which was powered by the further improved I-16 turbojets and was armed with a single 37-mm cannon and a pair of 0.50-in calibre machine guns in the nose.

Performance of the P-59 proved disappointing during evaluation with the USAAF 412th FG (Fighter Group), particularly in comparison to the first jet-powered fighters in Europe. Even the latest piston-engine fighter variants then in service performed better in many respects, including maximum speed and range. This resulted in only 66 aircraft being built, including prototype and service test aircraft.

YP-59A. USAF

Top: An YP-59 undergoing tests in the NACA Langley wind-tunnel. NASA **Centre:** This XP-59 is shown during evaluation with the USAAF 412th Fighter Group at Muroc. USAF **Above:** A handful of P-59's served with the USN, including this one with BuNo: 63960. The aircraft is shown before it was painted in a USN colour scheme. USN

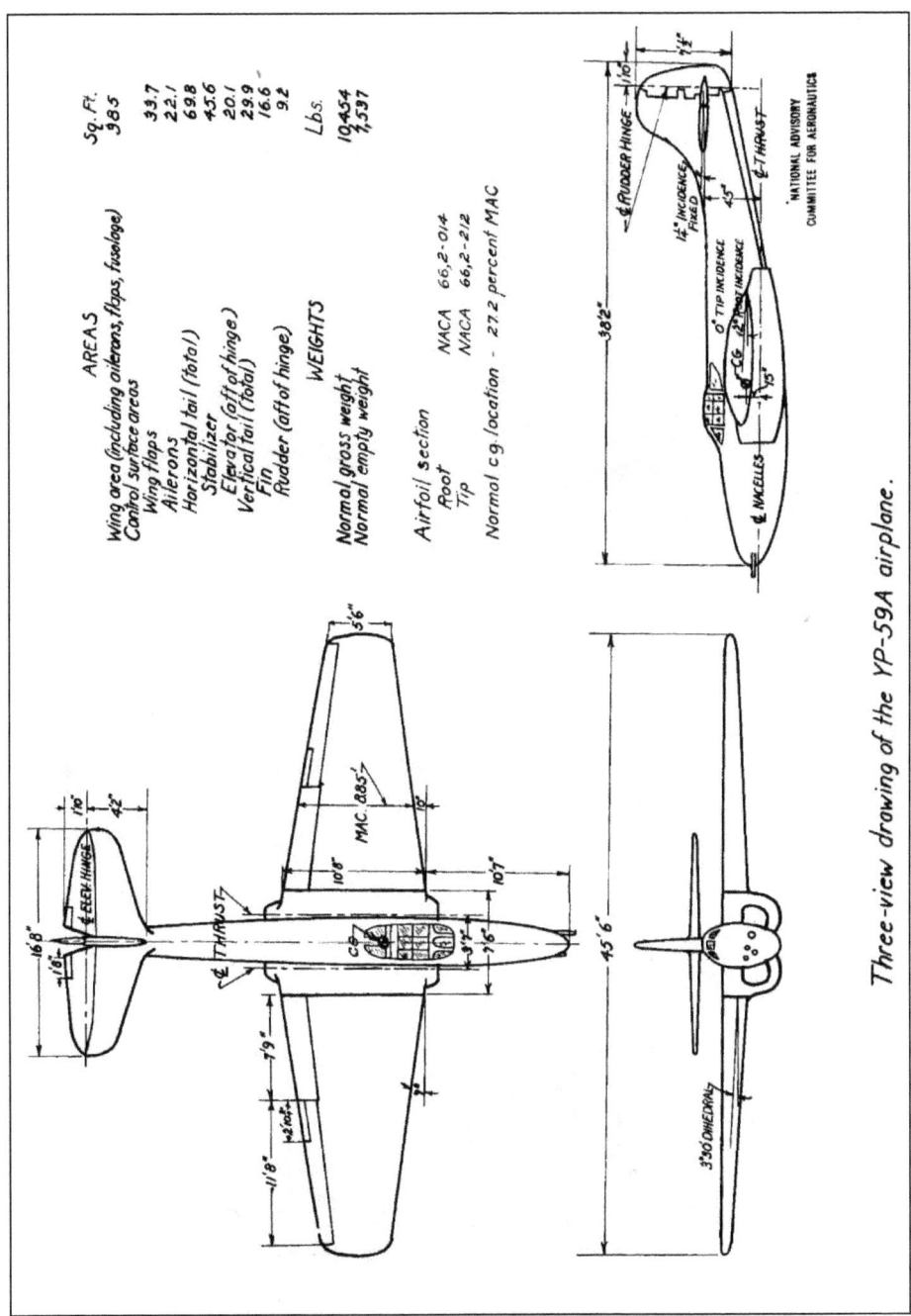

Three-view drawing of the YP-59A airplane.

Although lacking the performance to be a serious candidate for a front line service aircraft the P-59 proved invaluable in gaining experience in operation of jet-powered aircraft for the USAAF and the USAF, which succeeded it. Quickly overshadowed in the USAAF by the higher performing Lockheed P-80, the P-59 was relegated to a training aircraft status, while the P-80 went on to become the first operational jet fighter to enter service with the USAAF.

Top: The engines were mounted on the fuselage sides under the wings giving the aircraft a portly appearance. **Above;** This P-59B, S/N: 42-2633 is configured with drop fuel tanks typical of World War II fighter aircraft. **USAF**

The last variant of the small Airacomet family was the P-59B with 30 production aircraft built. This P-59B, S/N: 42-2650 shows the tricycle undercarriage arrangement and the low ground clearance of the type. USAF

Before retirement some P-59's were fitted with an open nose-cockpit for a second crewmember to house a drone control operator for the aircraft when tasked on drone control operations.

In late 1943, one aircraft was sent to the UK for evaluation in exchange for a Gloster Meteor F Mk. I twin-engine jet fighter. The Meteor was far more successful than its Bell counterpart, entering service with the RAF and seeing combat against Germany from July 1944. The Meteor went on to serve in successive variants with the RAF and many foreign air forces and saw combat in many post World War II conflicts including the Korean War and Arab Israeli conflicts where Meteor variants served on both sides.

XP-59A: 3 prototype aircraft with first flight of first aircraft being conducted on 1 October 1942
YP-59A: 13 service test aircraft with armament in nose
P-59A: 20 production aircraft for USAAF
P-59B: 30 production aircraft for USAAF

YP-59A

Engines: Two General Electric I-16 turbojets rated at 1,650-lb thrust each
Length: 38-ft 1.5-in
Height: 11-ft 11 ¾-in
Wingspan: 45-ft 6-in
Weights: 13,000-lb maximum gross
Maximum speed: 409-mph
Cruising speed: 320-mph
Service ceiling: 42,600-ft
Range: 440-miles

P-59B

Engines: Two General Electric I-16 turbojets rated at 1,650-lb thrust each
Length: 38-ft 10-in
Height: 11-ft 11 ¾-in
Wingspan: 45-ft 6-in
Weights: 10,532-lb fully loaded
Maximum speed: 409-mph (some figures quote a less realistic maximum speed of 450-mph, although it is accepted that maximum speed was 409-mph)
Cruising speed: 320-mph
Service ceiling: 43,400-ft
Range: 440-miles

Northrop XP-79 Flying Ram

The XP-79B was a truly unconventional fighter in both appearance and in one of its intended roles. The aircraft adopted a flying-wing configuration, albeit with twin-vertical tail surfaces. USAF

The Northrop XP-79 was initially designed as a rocket-powered interceptor aircraft with a number of novel features. The aircraft was a further development of the Northrop MX-334 rocket powered research aircraft, which was in turn developed from the MX-324, which was an unpowered glider. The MX-334 adopted the same basic airframe as the glider, but with changes to allow the accommodation of a small Aerojet XCAL-200 rocket engine. Like the MX-324 gliders, a Lockheed P-38 Lighting twin piston engine fighter towed the MX-334 into the air, with the first-flight taking place on 5 July 1944.

The design speed of the rocket powered MX-334 was only 300-mph, which was much slower than the 500+ mph being achieved by German rocket powered interceptors then entering service in the shape of the Messerschmitt Me.163 Komet. Ultimately, the MX-334 served only as a research tool and could never have been seriously considered as a practical military interceptor.

The XP-79B was developed from the MX-334 rocket powered research aircraft, which in turn was developed from the MX-324 glider seen above, all of which were designed to be towed into the air.

The pilot lay in the prone position, which theoretically enables the human body to be more tolerant to the stains of g-forces, which were unrealistically planned to be up to around 12-g in an operational P-79.

208915

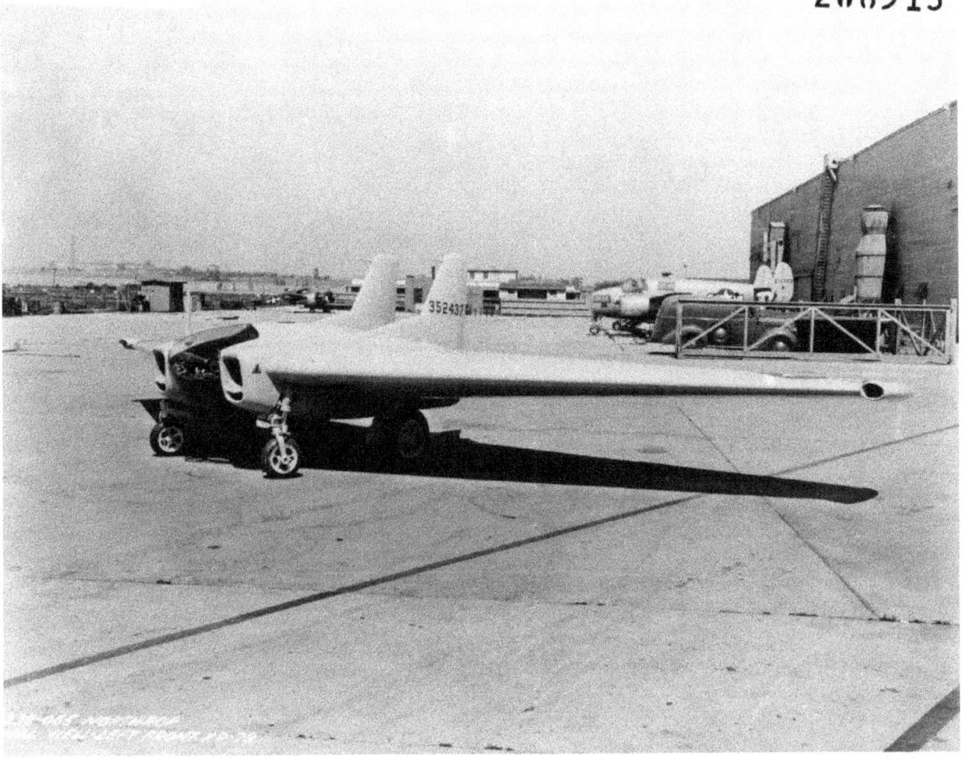

F

208914

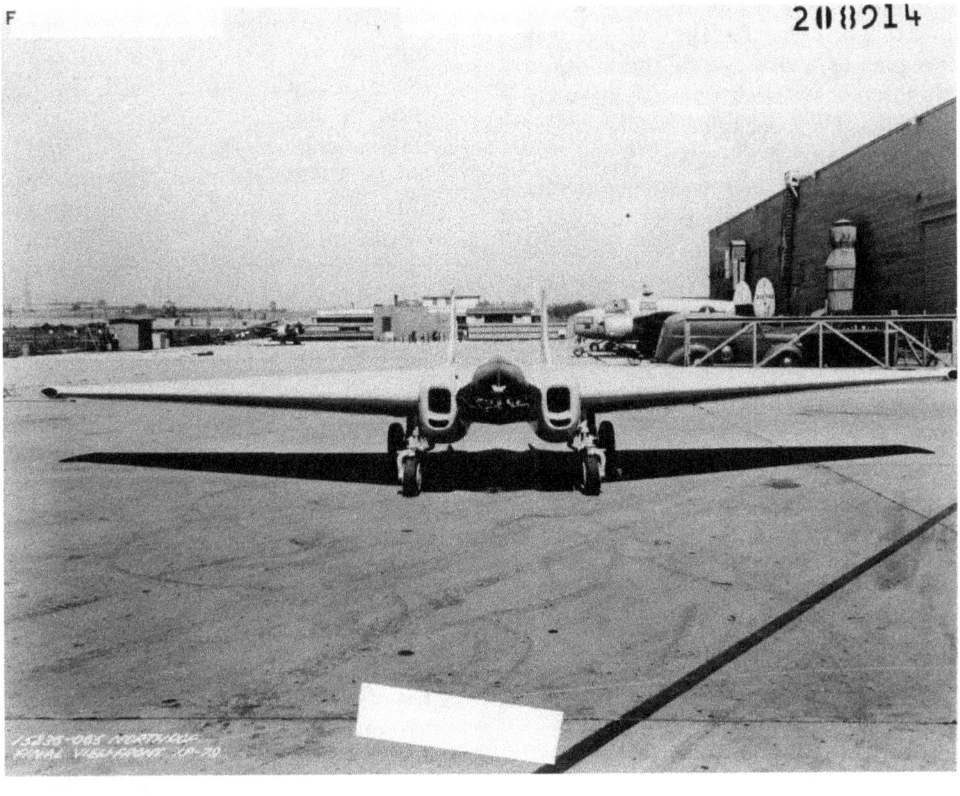

Previous page and above: Various views of the XP-79B. The side-on view above shows the flying wing configuration, spoilt only by the twin-vertical tail surfaces. USAF

Northrop and the USAAF, however, had not yet dropped the rocket powered interceptor concept. The XP-79 was designed as a flying-wing, building on Northrop's research into flying-wing aircraft. The cockpit at the front accommodated a pilot who lay in the prone position, which was theoretically designed to enable the pilot to sustain much higher g-forces of in excess of 12-g. However, in reality most if not all human beings would have been dead or at least in deep unconsciousness long before that figure was reached even when in the prone position. This type of pilot accommodation was not new. Germany had conducted studies and the Arado 234 Blitz jet reconnaissance/bomber aircraft, which entered operational service with the Luftwaffe in August 1944, housed its pilot in the prone position. Germany was also working on other prone position aircraft almost right up to the end of the war in Europe in May 1945.

Northrop received a contract for 3 rocket-powered XP-79's in January 1943, with work subsequently sub-contracted out to Avion Incorporated. The order for the rocket-powered XP-79 was cancelled as was the XP-79A rocket-powered aircraft. However, the program survived in the shape of the XP-79B, which was the third aircraft of the initial rocket powered XP-79 order, mow re-designed to be powered by turbojet-engines. .

The XP-79 received the nickname 'Flying Ram', as one planned role was for the aircraft to ram enemy bombers in the hope of slicing-off their tail sections. However, contrary to published accounts of the aircraft, ramming was not the aircraft's original design role and was never really taken seriously by the USAAF. The aircraft was designed as a conventionally armed interceptor carrying four 0.5-in heavy machine guns. The ramming was more of an afterthought; surprising since this type of operation can only be considered sane if conducted out of desperation to stop overwhelming forces. Since the US mainland was never placed in such a position and together with the other Allied forces was gaining the upper hand during the aircrafts development in World War II, the idea of expecting pilots to ram enemy aircraft as a matter of routine was to say the least ridiculous.

For ramming, the aircraft was to be built with a magnesium and steel structure, which it was claimed could survive at least several impacts with airborne aircraft. However, the idea was probably considered madness since even if the structure could survive the impact of ramming, debris from the rammed enemy bomber could easily be ingested in the air intakes for the turbojet engines, probably resulting in the loss of the aircraft.

This frontal upper view of the XP-79B's spinal area shows the cockpit and engine wells, which ran the entire length of the fuselage. USAF

Two Westinghouse J30-W-19B turbojet engines, each rated at around 1,150-lb thrust, powered the XP-79B. The two engines straddled the cockpit in the centre of the almost completely winged structure. Twin-vertical tail surfaces rose out of the extending engine bays and exhaust at the rear. The pilot lay in the prone position in a pressurised cockpit behind a Plexiglas cockpit canopy. The undercarriage consisted of two front and two rear wheels, which were located outboard of the engine bays; the wheels retracting outwards to lie in the wing.

The single XP-79B S/N: 43-52437 was delivered in June 1945, a few weeks after the end of the war in Europe. The aircraft had a short-lived career, being towed into the air for its first flight on 12 September 1945. The aircraft entered a roll from which the pilot was not able to recover and the aircraft subsequently crashed killing the pilot and bringing the XP-79B program to a sudden end.

The rocket powered XP-79 was dropped in favour of the XP-79B powered by twin turbojet engines. USAF

XP-79: 3 rocket-powered flying-wing interceptors; cancelled before any were built
XP-79A: Derivative of XP-79 rocket-powered interceptor - cancelled
XP-79B: 1 aircraft S/N: 43-52437 designed as a jet-powered flying-wing interceptor prototype

---

XP-79B

Engines: Two Westinghouse 19B turbojets each rated at 1,150 lb static thrust
Length: 14-ft 0-in
Height: 7-ft 6-in
Wingspan: 38-ft 0-in
Weights: 13,000-lb maximum gross
Maximum speed: 547 mph design speed 9mot achieved)
Crew: One

Lockheed F-80 Shooting Star

The Lockheed P-80 Shooting Star was the USAAF's first practical jet fighter suitable for operational use, with deliveries commencing in the weeks before the end World War II. AFFTC

The Lockheed P-80 (later F-80) Shooting Star was the best of the early jet fighters designed for the USAAF during World War II, ultimately becoming the first US aircraft to exceed 500-mph in level flight and the first jet fighter aircraft to enter operational service with the USAAF. Design of the aircraft began in 1943 by a Lockheed team headed by Chief designer Clarence L 'Kelly' Johnson, a name which would become legendary in aviation history with later designs including the U-2 and SR-71 Blackbird spy planes designed in the 1950's and 1960's.

The Shooting Star program, like all of the US's early jets, benefited from the wealth of technical data and assistance passed over from Britain. As the United States was trailing behind Britain in jet propulsion technology, and had nothing even remotely suitable to power the USAAF's fledgling jet fighter programs. The 32-ft long XP-80, named 'Lulu Belle' by personnel at Lockheed, was powered by a British de Havilland Halford H-1B turbojet rated at 2,460-lb st thrust, with the airframe more or less designed around the engine. The aircraft adopted a conventional configuration with straight wings, a single vertical tail and conventional horizontal tail-planes and rudder. Two small air intakes were located on the lower sides of the fuselage to feed the engines, which occupied more or less the entire rear fuselage, which detached for engine maintenance or changes. The cockpit was located behind the solid nose section, which would house the gun armament in production aircraft.

The design team created the basic aircraft in 143 days, which although much lauded and certainly a short period, was hardly remarkable for the

The XP-80 was smaller than the intended production variant, merely acting as a demonstrator aircraft.

time, considering the Germans were churning our jet fighters designs from drawing board to first flight in a matter of weeks. Furthermore, the Americans had the nicety of ready made British turbojets for their new fighter and a manufacturing program free from the inconveniencies of constant air attack and harassment, which the Germans and to a much lesser extent the British had to contend with.

The XP-80 conducted its maiden flight on 8 January 1944 and attained a speed of 490-mph. Just over one month later the XP-80 exceeded 500-mph during official USAAF acceptance tests at Muroc.

Although the design was always aimed at fielding an operational jet powered fighter the single XP-80 was merely an aerodynamic test-bed for a larger aircraft and was followed by three XP-80A's powered by an Allison J33, which was effectively a licence built de-Havilland Goblin used in the British de Havilland Vampire F Mk. I jet fighter.

The first XP-80A conducted its maiden flight at Muroc on 10 June 1944, and during the test program achieved speeds of well over 500-mph.

Top right: The single XP-80, named 'Lullu belle' was powered by a single British de Havilland Halford H-1B turbojet rated at 2,460-lb static thrust. Above: The single XP-80 was followed by a batch of 3 XP-80A's. USAF

P-80A 48-5099 operating with NACA as a test aircraft on 22 July 1946. NASA Ames

During suitability testing the XP-80A's were used to prove that the design could successfully engage enemy bomber formations; hardly a priority at the time, with the war in Europe and the Far East going in favour of the Allies, which faced a negligible threat from enemy bombers. Further tests showed that in high-speed fights the XP-80A's could outperform the best USAAF piston engine fighters. Satisfied with the XP-80A's performance, the USAAF accepted the design for production.

The XP-80A's were followed by a batch of 13 YP-80A's used for service evaluation before full-scale production of the P-80A commenced. The first production P-80A was delivered in February 1945. However, production was slow and only handfuls of early P-80A's entered service with the USAAF before the end of the WW II. A few were sent to USAAF units in the UK and Italy for evaluation, although at the time of the German surrender the P-80A was far from capable of being assessed as a credible combat force. Unlike the first German and British operational jet fighters, the P-80 did not see combat in WW II.

Test carried out post war showed that the maximum speed of the P-80A was 526 mph at 12,000 ft and maximum cruising speed was 434 mph at 24,000 ft, although different tests gave different figures dependant on the aircraft used, engine used and aircraft configuration. A post war evaluation document, Report No. F-TR-1133-ND by US Air Material Command found that "Despite a difference in gross weight of nearly 2000 lb, the Me-262 (Me.262)... was superior to the average Lockheed P-80A in acceleration and speed, and approximately the same in climb performance. In conclusion the P-80A was, despite entering service a year and a half later, inferior to the basic Me.262. It should be noted, however, that developed variants of the Me.262 would have been expected to push the performance margin over the P-80A still further. Comparing the British Gloster Meteor III with the Me.262, a 1945 RAE report stated that with engines of equal thrust the Meteor III would be 20 mph slower than the Me.262. It also stated that the Meteors lower wing loading gave it better manoeuvrability than the Me.262.

Top: This almost plan study of a P-80 in flight shows to effect the aircraft's small size. This aircraft, which appears to have the serial number 48-5004, is fitted with the characteristic wingtip fuel tanks. AFFTC. Above: P-80A 48-5099 operating with NACA as a test aircraft, fitted with instrumentation for its flight test role. NASA Ames

Top: An XP-80A test-ship flies over the dry lakebed at Muroc in the 1940's. The first XP-80A flew on 1 June 1944 followed by the second on 1 August that year. The XP-80A's were followed by 13 YP-80A's; the first of which conducted its maiden flight on 13 September 1944, being accepted by the USAAF five days later. AFFTC Above:-P-80A 45-8480 in flight over mountainous terrain. The code on the nose commencing with 'P' reverted to a code commencing with 'F' once the 'P' for pursuit designation changed to 'F' for fighter in 1948. USAF

P-80A 44-85231 conducts a Rocket Assisted Take-off. USAF

Production of the P-80A numbered 917, used as a nucleus of USAAF (later USAF) first generation jet fighter units. The P-80B designation covered 240 aircraft (moved from P-80A production) powered by a J36 turbojet.

This P-80/F-80 was operated by NACA on various test programs. NASA Ames

The next major production variant was the P-80C, 798 of which were produced. This variant saw extensive combat service over Korea during the June 1950 to July 1953 Korean War, by which time it had been re-designated F-80 in line with the change from P (Pursuit) to F (Fighter) in 1948. Early in that conflict the F-80 was the most advanced fighter operated by either side and had more or less free range over Korea. However, the introduction by Communist forces of the Soviet designed MiG-15 swept wing jet fighter changed this, with the inferior F-80 unable to cope with the MiG's. The USAF claimed that an F-80C shot down a MiG-15 in the first ever jet versus jet air combat engagement on 8 November 1950, however, data from the other side claims that a Soviet flown MiG-15 shot down an F-80C a week earlier on 1 November, which now appears to probably be the first manned jet versus jet air combat. F-80C S/N 49-593 was lost over Korea on 1 November 1950 supporting communist claims. Victories over the MiG-15 would prove to be few and far between as the F-80C was outclassed in the air-to-air arena, but found its true niche as a fighter-bomber supporting United Nations ground forces. During the war 285 F-80's were lost.

P-80A S/N: 44-85044 was used as a test aircraft, modified to carry a pair of 0.50 calibre machine guns housed in the upper nose. The guns could be deflected to various angles for the deflection tests, which were aimed at developing ways to shoot down enemy bombers from a position behind and below the target aircraft. Similar systems had been used operationally by German Night Fighters against RAF bombers in the later stages of World War II. USAF

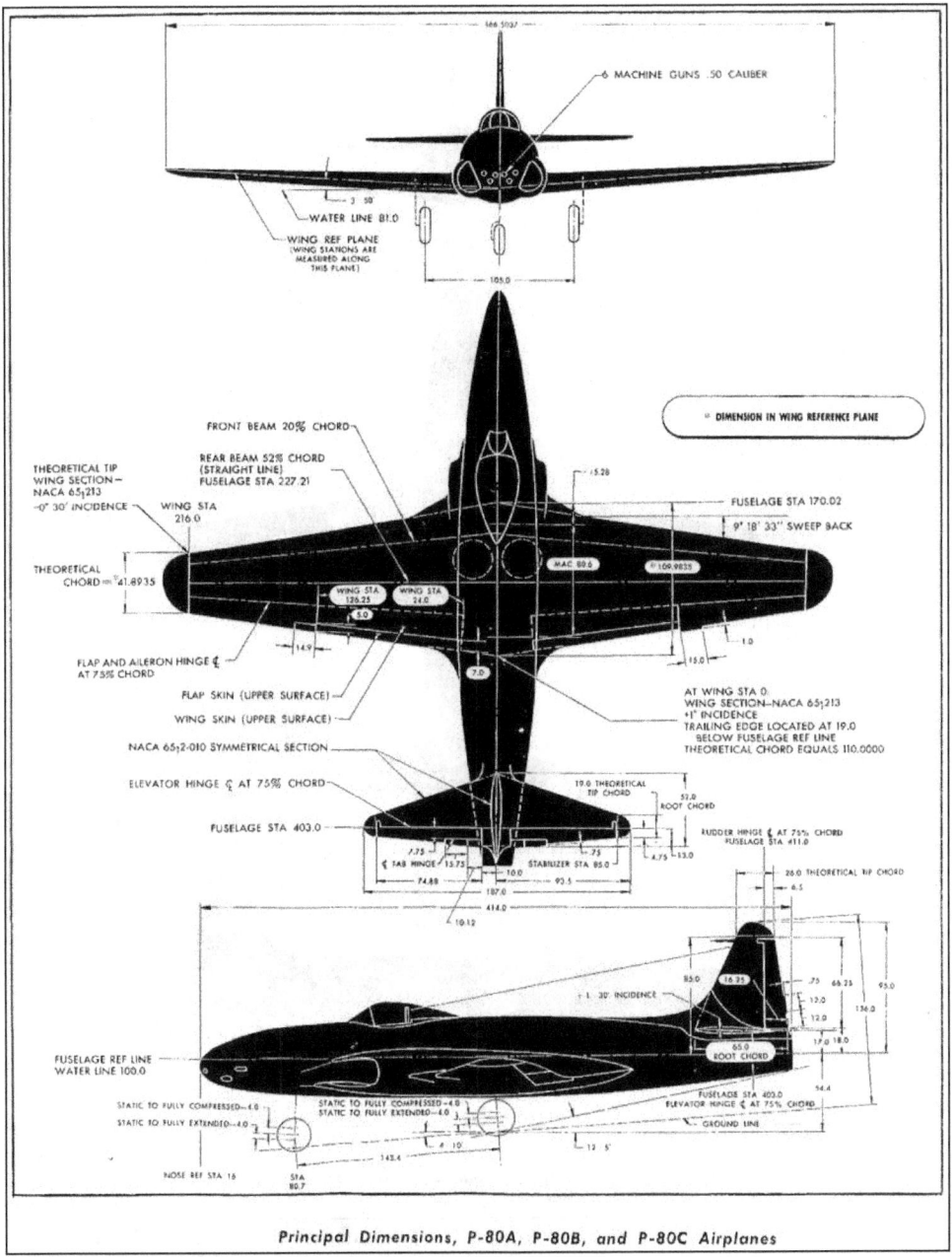

Principal Dimensions, P-80A, P-80B, and P-80C Airplanes

Extraversion

Four of the XP-80A's were transferred to Europe under the "Extraversion" operation, which was an evaluation program to be conducted under European/Mediterranean conditions. This program which ended in May 1945 is often misinterpreted as having been a combat evaluation; a fallacy that has endured more than 70 years. Two the four aircraft deployed under this program were lost in accidents and the others were returned to the US when the program ended; being integrated into various test programs. One of the two aircraft lost during the Extraversion program had been re-engined with a Rolls Royce B-41 turbojet.

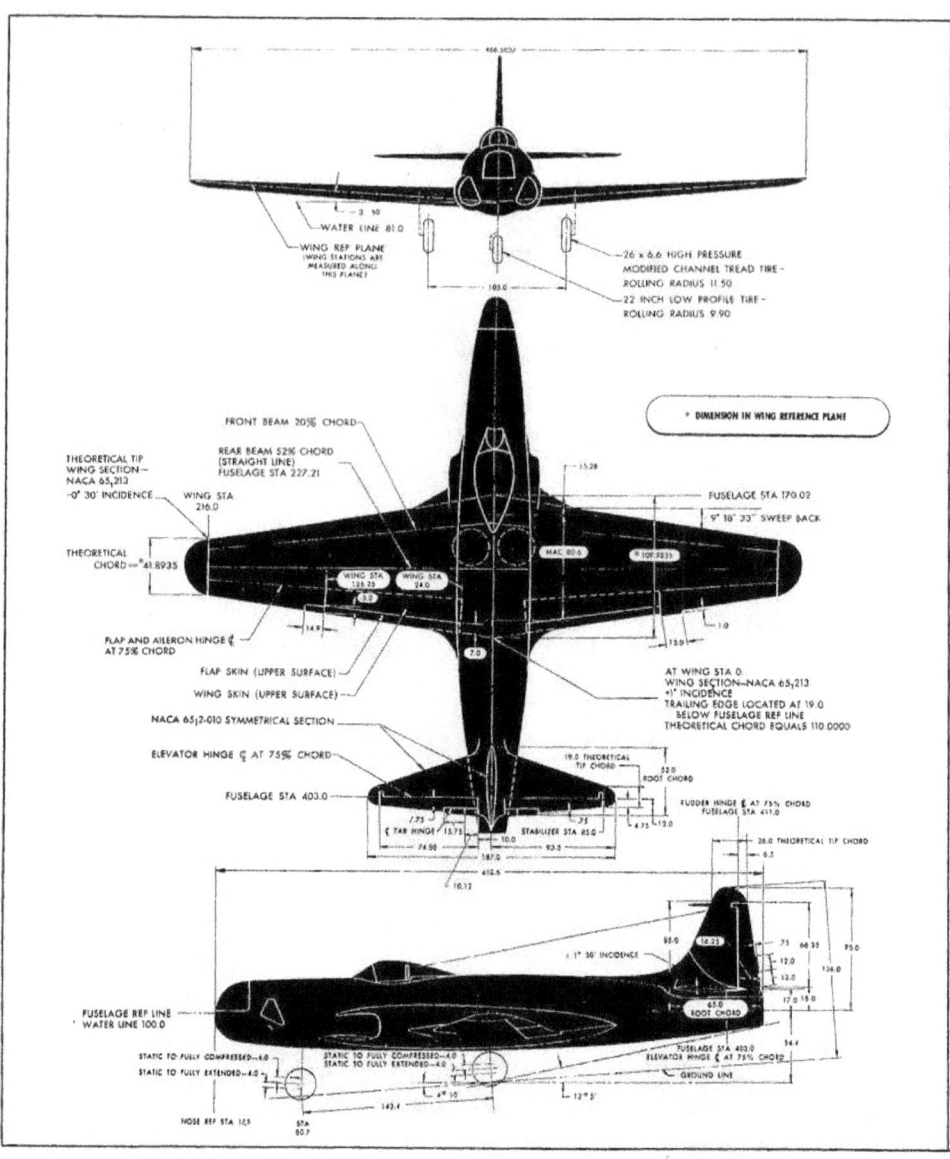

Principal Dimensions, FP-80A Airplanes

Ordered in early 1944, the XP-80A's were flown on 1 June and 1 August 1944. The second aircraft was used to flight test the General Electric I-40 (later re-designated J33-11) turbojet. The first of the 13 YP-80A's conducted its maiden flight on 13 September 1944 and was accepted by the USAAF on the 18th. The second YP-80A was built as the XF-14, which was effectively the prototype of what would become the RF-80. On 2 April 1944, prior to the first flight of an XP-80A, the USAAF decided to proceed with a P-80A order for two batches of 500 aircraft each. In June 1945 a further contract raised the total order to over 3,500 aircraft; the majority subsequently cancelled with the end of the war. The first P-80A conducted its maiden flight in February 1945, with 917 being delivered, the last 12 being received in December 1946. The 412th FG began receiving aircraft in 1945 and was declared operational in 1946. Less than 600 P-80A's entered USAAF service, with 152 of the 917 aircraft being delivered as FP-80A (later RF-80) and a further 70 were converted from F-80A's, with 98 being re-engined with J33-35's in 1953. 240 of the 917 aircraft were delivered as P-80B's. Total deliveries of all models would reach 1,731.

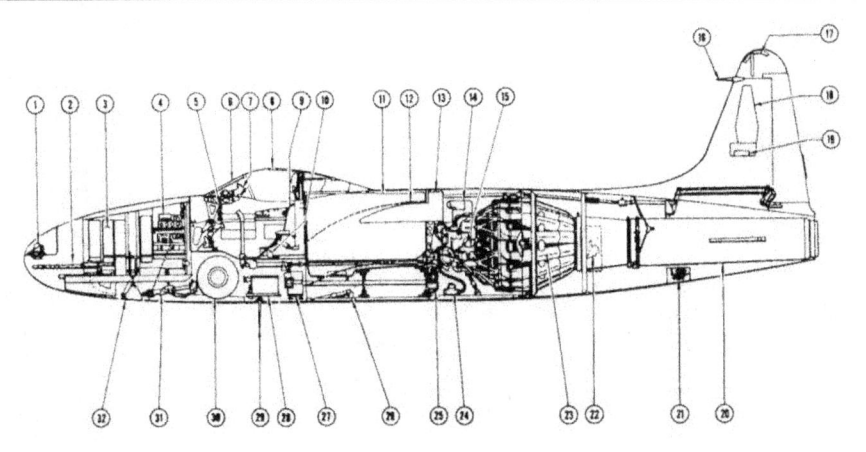

1. AN/ARN-6 Radio Compass Loop Antenna
2. 50 Calibre Machine Guns (6)
3. Ammunition Boxes (6)
4. AN/ARC-3 and AN/ARN-6 Radio
5. Instrument Panel
6. Bullet Proof Windshield Panel
7. Gun Sight
8. AN/ARN-6 Radio Sense Antenna
9. Pilot's Seat
10. "G" Valve
11. Fuselage Fuel Tank
12. Intake Air Duct
13. Water Tank
14. Turbo-Refrigerator
15. Engine Control Valve (Throttle)
16. Air Speed Pitot
17. AN/ARC-3 Radio Pick Axe Antenna
18. AN/ARA-8A Radio Antenna
19. AN/ARA-8A Radio Homing Device
20. Tailpipe
21. Gyrosyn Compass Flux Valve
22. Elevator Tab Motor
23. Engine
24. Fuel Flowmeter
25. Aileron Booster Unit
26. Dive Recovery Flaps
27. SCR-695-A Radio
28. Battery
29. SCR-695-A Radio Antenna
30. Nose Landing Gear
31. Landing and Taxi Lights
32. Case Ejection Door

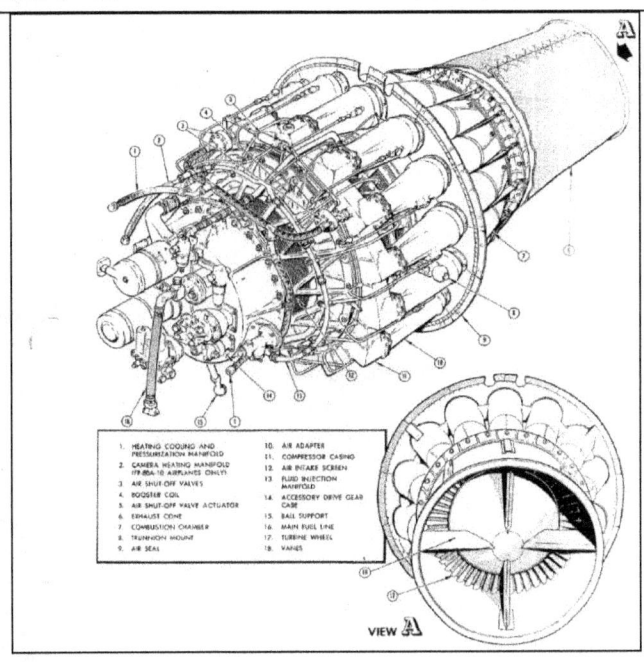

1. HEATING COOLING AND PRESSURIZATION MANIFOLD
2. CAMERA HEATING MANIFOLD (TF-80A-10 AIRPLANES ONLY)
3. AIR SHUT-OFF VALVES
4. BOOSTER COIL
5. AIR SHUT-OFF VALVE ACTUATOR
6. EXHAUST CONE
7. COMBUSTION CHAMBER
8. TRUNNION MOUNT
9. AIR SEAL
10. AIR ADAPTER
11. COMPRESSOR CASING
12. AIR INTAKE SCREEN
13. FLUID INJECTION MANIFOLD
14. ACCESSORY DRIVE GEAR CASE
15. BALL SUPPORT
16. MAIN FUEL LINE
17. TURBINE WHEEL
18. VANES

VIEW A

Top: A batch of P-80A's with 44-85226 in the foreground is prepared for delivery to Chanute Air Force Base on 19 May 1946. Above: A trio of F-80A's, 44-85313, 44-85280 and 44-85274. While the P-80A was powered by either the General Electric J33-11 or the Allison J33-9, which were interchangeable, from the 346th aircraft the Allison J33-17 was installed, with the earlier engines reworked to -17 standard. In a program to introduce some features of the P-80B, all in-service P-80A's were equipped with under wing rockets launchers and most received an engine water alcohol injection system and some other minor modifications.
USAF

Top: At the start of the Korean War this F-80C was operating with the 8th FBG (Fighter Bomber Group) in Japan. The aircraft is now displayed at the National Museum of the USAF (centre and above). USAF

The F-80 was widely used by the USAF during the Korean War. This quartet of F-80's is from the 8th FBW (Fighter Bomber Wing). US DoD

Prior to the start of the Korean War in June 1950, six ANG (Air National Guard) squadrons flew the F-80C, but relinquished the jet fighters that same year as they were required for USAF active duty units. Following the Korean War, F-80C's equipped 22 ANG squadrons with the last Shooting Star being retired from ANG service in 1958, having been retired from active USAF service earlier. ANG units flew the RF-80A during the Korean War, but converted to piston engine North American F-51 Mustangs when they returned to state control in the US in 1954. Post Korean War, RF-80A's equipped a further five ANG squadrons with the last aircraft being retired from ANG service in 1961.

As the USAF's first practical jet fighter with a speed in excess of the best piston engine fighters available, it was natural that a tactical reconnaissance variant of the Shooting Star would be developed. Initially designated F-14A, the tactical reconnaissance variant was re-designated FP-80A and finally RF-80C, with a 114 aircraft delivered.

An armoured loads the 6 x 0.50 calibre machine gun primary armament of a Fifth Air Force F-80C in Korea. Note the upwards hinging side panels giving access the guns. USAF

Previous page top: At the start of the Korean War the F-80 was used to intercept the obsolete World War II era Russian built Yak piston engine fighters and an assortment of other obsolete propeller driven aircraft of the North Korean Air Force. It was not until November 1950 and the advent of MiG-15 operations, that the F-80C came up wanting in performance. Previous page bottom: RF-80's were used for the reconnaissance mission in Korea, providing invaluable intelligence such as this pre-landing photo of Inchon on 31 August 1950. This page top: A line of F-80's at Itazuke, Japan during the Korean War in 1950. The F-80's are from the 8th FBG, while the F-82 in the foreground is from the 69th AWFS (All Weather Fighter Squadron). Above: An F-80C with a pair of 1,000 lb bombs and external drop tanks on the wingtips. USAF

Top: RF-80's operating in Korea were painted in an olive drab scheme to make them less conspicuous to Communist MiG-15 fighters. Above: An RF-80 shot this low level photo of the Suiho dam in Korea. USAF

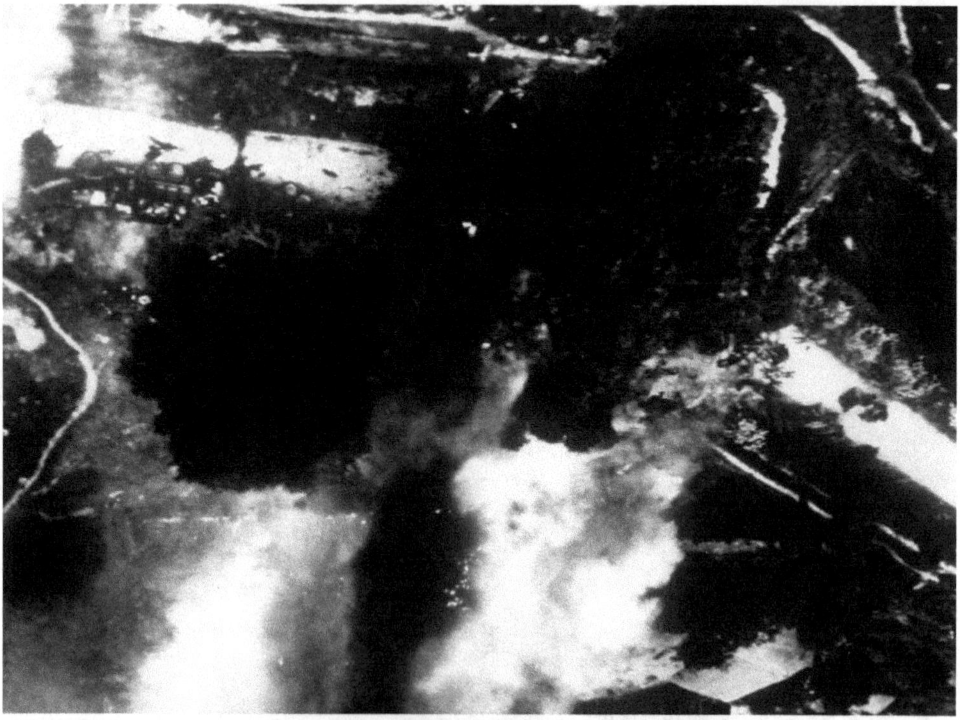

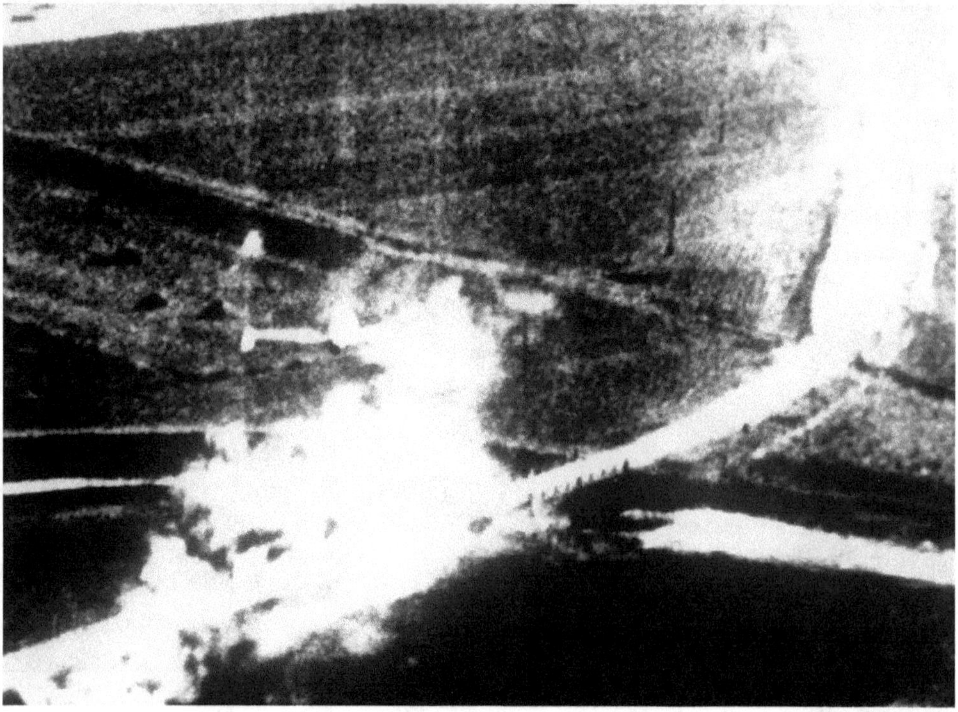

Previous page top: Following the advent of the MiG-15 in the Korean Theatre the F-80 was outclassed in the air to air role. As increasing numbers of North American F-86 Sabres appeared, the F-80 was increasingly employed in the air to surface role. Here an F-80 beats up a North Korean convoy at Tuman, 10 miles south east of Kongju South Korea Bottom: F-80's strafe a North Korean convoy just north of the 38th Parallel. Above: A four-ship formation of F-80's from the 9th FBW during the Korean War. US DoD

Top: Four of the main USAF fighter types employed in Korea. Clockwise from rear: F-86; F-80; F-82 and F-84. Centre: An F-80 Radio Command and Drone Control aircraft is seen with a drone configured aircraft. Above: Displayed at the National Museum of the USAF, the F-80R was used to break the world air speed record. USAF

The basic Shooting Star design was also used for a variety of other roles including the T-33 jet trainer, which was initially developed under the designation TF-80C, primarily as a conversion trainer for the F-80. Some T-33A's were converted to RT-33A for use in the reconnaissance role with export nations such as Taiwan, which lost a number to PLAAF (Peoples Liberation Army Air Force) MiG's and ground defences.

T-33A's were also transferred to the USN under the designation TV-2, with an advanced variant of the T-33A designated T2V-1 also being procured by the USN. The USAF also transferred a number of F-80C's to the USN under the designation TV-1. Large numbers of F-80's and T-33's were converted to QF-80F and QT-33B target drone configuration following retirement from operational use. A number of other minor and one off conversions were undertaken for the USAF and USN.

An F-80 from the 51st FIW conducts a JATO (Jet Assisted Take-Off) take-off in May 1951. US DoD

In the immediate post WW II years the absolute world air speed record was held by Great Britain, which captured the record in a Gloster Meteor IV jet fighter. The USAAF planned to capture the record with a modified P-80 designated P-80R. This aircraft, S/N 44-85200 was extensively modified including the fitting of a smaller cockpit canopy, shorter span wing with extended leading edge and redesigned engine air intakes and a J33-A-21engine rated at 5,079-lb thrust. The aircraft had a service ceiling of 45,000 ft and a range of 1,045 miles. All armament was removed and the space occupied by an additional fuel tank. To increase ballistic aerodynamics all openings, which could produce drag were sealed over. The P-80R captured the record with a speed of 623.753-mph during a flight at Muroc Dry Lake (now Edwards AFB), California on 19 June 1947. Although this had returned the record to the US after 24 years, it had been achieved using a jet engine based on British technology, probably damping the achievement a little. The P-80R was transferred from Griffiss AFB, New York to the USAF Museum in October 1954.

Top right: In 1948 the USAF buzz codes changed from 'P' for pursuit to 'F' for fighter class aircraft. Above: This quartet of F-80's is shown in tight formation devoid of wingtip fuel tanks. USAF

The F-80C and RF-80 were widely used during the Korean War in which 285 were reported lost to a number of causes including ground fire and air-to-air losses. These 2 F-80C's are getting airborne for an air to surface mission armed with a pair of 1,000-lb bombs each. US DoD **Below:** The EF-80A was a conversion from F-80A production aircraft. The forward nose section was converted to house an additional cockpit for a drone controller. USAF

XP-80: 1 prototype powered by a British Halford H-1B turbojet
XP-80A: 3 aircraft powered by a General Electric J33-GE-5 turbojet

YP-80A: 13 service test aircraft consisting of 12 new build and 1 conversion from the XP-80A
F-80A: 525 aircraft delivered to USAAF from 1,000 ordered in 1944. The F-80A was phased out of active service from October 1951.
RF-80: 152 aircraft from the 1,000 P-80A's ordered in April 1944 were delivered as FP-80A (RF-80A) and a further 70 were converted from F-80A's. The RF-80 remained in active service until 1957.
XF-80B: 1 (conversion) later converted to P-80R for speed record attempt.
F-80B: 240 initially designated P-80Z powered by Allison J33-21. These aircraft were part of the 1944 contract for 1,000 P-80A's but were delivered as P-80B's. The first aircraft was accepted as a P-80Z on 7 March 1947, being designated P-80B the following month. Production of the P-80B ended in March 1948 and the aircraft commenced its phase out from active service in 1951.

The P-80R makes a high-speed run at Muroc. AFFTC

F-80C: 798 production aircraft similar to F-80A/B ordered, but only 670 accepted as F-80C's by the USAF. The Remaining 128 were delivered as TF-80C/T-33's. The Last USAF F-80C unit relinquished its aircraft around March 1954 and the aircraft was retired from ANG service in 1958.

TF-80C/T-33: 128 aircraft initially ordered as F-80C's were delivered as TF-80C's. In August 1947 a P-80C was taken from the production line and modified, which included a 38.8 in fuselage extension to accommodate a second seat in the lengthened cockpit. This aircraft was designated TF-80C in June 1948, having conducted its maiden flight on 22 March that year, at which time it was still known as the TP-80C. These training aircraft were re-designated T-33 on 5 May 1949.

XP-80
Engine: 1 de Havilland Halford H-1B turbojet rated at 2,460-lb st thrust
Length: 32-ft 10-in
Wingspan: 37-ft
Weights: 8,916-lb gross
Maximum speed: 502-mph
Service ceiling: 41,000-ft

F-80C
Engine: A single Allison J33 turbojet rated at 5,400-lb thrust (with alcohol water injection). The P-80R was powered by an Allison J33-A-23 turbojet rated at 5,079-lb thrust (with alcohol water injection)
Length: 34-ft 6-in
Height: 11-ft 4-in
Wingspan: 38-ft 10.5-in (P-80R had a wingspan of 37 ft)
Weights: 16,856-lb maximum take-off (P-80R had a maximum take-off weight of 12,054 lb; almost 5,000 lb lower than the F-80C)
Maximum speed: 579-mph at 7,000 ft
Cruising speed: 437-mph
Service ceiling: 46,800-ft
Range: 1,090-miles

Consolidated Vultee XP-81

The Consolidated Vultee XP-81 was one of a number of experimental fighter designs, which attempted to combine the performance of a turbojet, with the range/economy of a turboprop, into an operational fighter. USAF

The Consolidated Vultee XP-81 emerged from a requirement to overcome the extremely limited range of first generation jet fighters. The XP-81 was an attempt to solve the problem by using two separate engines; an Allison J33 turbojet rated at 3,750-lb thrust would be used during take-off and air combat, while a 1,650-hp General Electric XT-31 gas-turbine turboprop would be used during cruise flight as turboprops were much more fuel efficient than turbojets. The turboprop engine drove a large four bladed propeller positioned in the nose.

The aircraft was a single-crew conventional straight mid-set wing with conventional vertical and horizontal tail surfaces. The tricycle undercarriage consisted of a single nose-wheel, which retracted aft to lie in the forward fuselage and single main wheels, which retracted inwards to be housed in the inner wing section.

The first XP-81 S/N 44-91000 sits on the ramp at Muroc in 1945. USAF

The USAAF ordered a pair of XP-81's with S/N 44-91000 and 44-91001 on 11 February 1944 and the first of these conducted its maiden flight almost one year later on 7 February 1945. However, delays with development of the intended XT-31 turboprop meant that the prototype flew with a Packard built British Rolls Royce Merlin V-1650 piston engine. Once the XT-31 was ready the first XP-81 was retrofitted and flew for the first time with this engine fitted on 21 December 1945. However, the new turboprop provided hardly any performance advantage over the Merlin piston engine. Moreover, the performance was considered to be

When flown with the planned turboprop engine, the XP-81 showed little improvement in performance compared with flying with the Merlin piston engine. The XP-81 had a cruising speed of 275-mph when flown under the power of the turboprop and the J33 turbojet shut down. USAFM

generally poor overall, leaving the USAAF unimpressed, leading to cancellation of an order for 13 YP-81's. The 2 XP-81's were used for test purposes until retired from flying duties on 29 September 1947 when they were declared obsolete. Although proving to be inadequate for the fighter role, the XP-81's laid claim to a number of firsts including the first turboprop powered fighter for the USAAF as well as the USAAF's first turbojet/piston and turbojet/turboprop combination fighter.

XP-81: 2 aircraft S/N 44-91000 and 44-91001 ordered under an initial contract on 18 January 1944

YP-81: 13 (some documentation suggests 11) aircraft ordered for service test program, but subsequently cancelled.

The first XP-81 flew on 7 February 1945 (some documentation suggests 11 February 1945); the two aircraft conducting 89 hours and 45 minutes of flight between them.

P-81A (Planned)

Engines: an Allison J33 turbojet rated at 3,750-lb thrust and a General Electric T-31 turboprop developing 1,650-hp (as the XT-31 engine was not ready a Packard built Rolls Royce Merlin V-1650 was used for initial flight testing).
Length: 44-ft 10-in
Height: 14-ft 0-in
Wingspan: 50-ft 6-in
Weights: 24,650-lb maximum take-off
Maximum speed: 507-mph (planned)
Cruising speed: 275-mph (under turboprop power only)
Service ceiling: 35,500-ft
Range: 2,500-miles

Previous page and this page: The principal aim of the XP-81 mixed power plant fighter was to try and overcome the major problem of low endurance of the early jet fighters. The USN adopted a similar program with the Ryan FR-1 Fireball. While these designs could overcome the short-range to a certain degree, they were never really practical as the aircraft was burdened with the weight of an additional engine, which had seriously detrimental effect on aircraft performance, therefore, the XP-81 was ultimately doomed to cancellation due to the impracticality of the design for operational service. USAF

Bell XP-83

The first of two XP-83 prototypes built for the USAAF, 44-84990 flew for the first time on 25 February 1945. USAF

The Bell XP-83 emerged from a desire to introduce a jet powered fighter aircraft with improved performance over the disappointing Bell P-59 Aircacomet. As it was obvious from the start that the Bell P-59 design would be outperformed by jet fighters entering service and under development in Europe and even by the latest generation of piston engine fighters, it was decided to embark upon an improved design, which emerged as the Bell XP-83 This new design was an outgrowth of the P-59, featuring a pressurised cockpit and designed as a possible escort fighter.

Emphasis was placed on extending range, which was extremely poor in the P-59, as it was in most early jets. The XP-83 was a larger aircraft than the P-59, although wingspan was slightly shorter. Maximum take-off weight was over 24,000-lb compared with the P-59B's relatively lightweight showing in comparison at just over 10,500-lb maximum take-off. The XP-83 was powered by a pair of Allison J33 turbojet engines, which were located close to the aircraft's centreline as a safety feature as in the event of a single engine failure the other engine would not cause as serious a control problem because of asymmetrical thrust. The engines were accommodated against the fuselage sides under the wings. The airframe housed large internal fuel tanks containing 1,150 gallons of fuel giving the aircraft a substantial range increase over the P-59. As the aircraft was designed for operations at altitudes above 40,000-ft a pressurised cockpit was incorporated. Like the P-59, production standard P-83's would have housed a 0.5-in machine gun and or cannon armament in the nose and production aircraft would possibly have been armed with air to surface stores including bombs and unguided rockets.

The XP-83 did little to improve on the disappointment of the P-59, which combined with the aircrafts huge weight led to the programs cancellation. USAF

Under an initial contract of 11 March 1944, 2 XP-83's were ordered with serial numbers 44-84990 and 44-84991. The first of these flew for the first time on 25 February 1945. Although powered by more powerful engines than the P-59 the XP-83 ultimately became far too heavy and offered little if anything of an improvement over in-service fighter aircraft resulting in the programs cancellation without entering production.

The portly looks of the XP-83 are clearly evident in these photographs of the first prototype 44-84990. The top photographs shows the XP-83 next to a Lockheed P-80, although from the angle, the size contrast is not obvious, although at 24,090-lb, the XP-83 was in the order of twice the weight of a P-80. USAF

XP-83: 2 aircraft S/N 44-84990 and 44-84991 powered by two Allison J33 turbojets. Designed as a high altitude escort fighter, the P-83 ultimately became too heavy resulting in it being grossly underpowered.

Specification

XP-83

Engines: Two Allison J-33 turbojets
Length: 44-ft 10-in
Height: 14-ft 0-in
Wingspan: 43-ft 0-in
Weights: 24,090-lb maximum take-off
Maximum speed: 525-mph (planned)
Service ceiling: 45,000-ft
Range: 1,580-miles (increased to 2,000-miles with external fuel tanks)

Republic F-84 Thunderjet

The XP-84, above, adopted a relatively simple design approach with a simple nose air intake feeding the turbojet engine. AFFTC

The Republic Corporation became a major name in the US fighter aircraft industry with the beefy P-47 Thunderbolt, which along with the North American P-51 Mustang was the mainstay of the USAAF single-engine fighter forces in the later stages of WW II. With the world of aviation taking strides into the jet era towards the end of WW II, the USAAF wanted to introduce a number of tactical jet fighters to operational service.

Development of the XP-84 began in 1944 and three XP-84 prototypes were ordered in March 1945, with the design being refined in the months following the end of WW II. The XP-84 emerged as a simple straight wing aircraft powered by a single J35 (licence built de Havilland Goblin) turbojet engine.

The XP-84's were powered by a General Electric J35-GE-7 rated at 3,750-lb (7.6-kN) static thrust. Unlike the Lockheed P-80 Shooting Star, which had lateral fuselage mounted intakes, the XP-84 adopted a simple nose mounted intake, which fed air directly to the engine housed in the rear fuselage with the jet pipe at the extreme rear.

The first XP-84 during an early development flight showing the bulky forward fuselage. USAF

These two photographs of XP-84 45-59475, which was the first of the XP-84's built, clearly shows the simple straightforward design of the aircraft. The design of the aircraft commenced in 1944 and the XP-84 aircraft were ordered in March the following year. These aircraft were powered by the General Electric J35-GE-7 turbojet engine, which was basically a licence built variant of the British de Havilland Goblin turbojet. The J35-GE-7 was rated at 3,750-lb (7.6 kN) static thrust. USAF

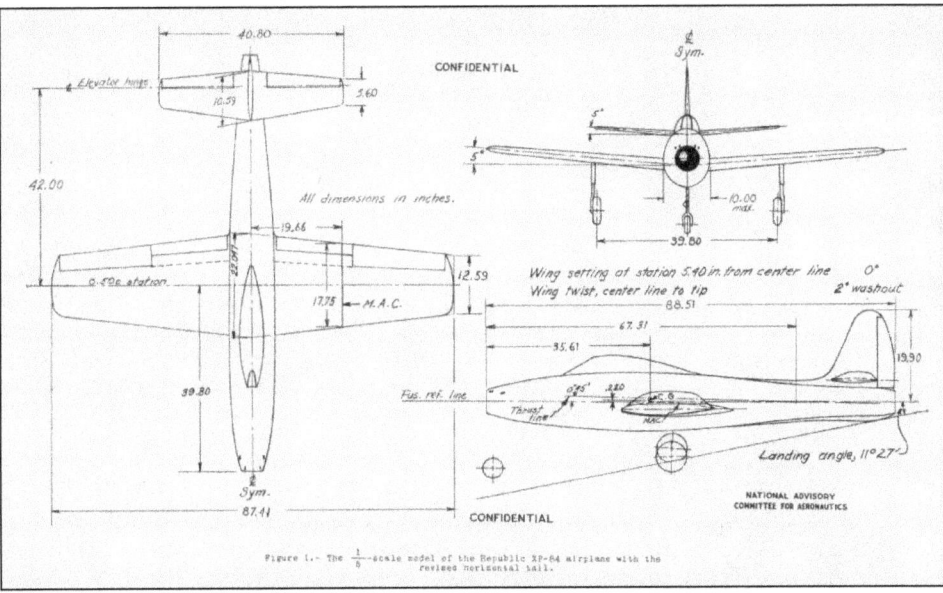

GOR (General Operational Requirement), issued on 11 September 1944 specified a day fighter featuring mid-set wings with a top speed of 600 mph, a combat radius of 850 miles armed with either 8 x 0.50 calibre or 6 x 0.60 calibre machine guns; this requirement later being reduced to either 6 x 0.50 or 4 x 0.60 calibre guns. The aircrafts required radius of action was also reduced to 705 miles. The go-ahead was ordered on 11 November 1944, followed on 4 January 1945 by a Letter of contract, for a USAAF order for 25 service test aircraft and 75 production aircraft designated P-84. The order was later changed to 15 YP-84A's, and 85 P-84B's. On 12 March 1945 a definitive contract was signed for three aircraft designated XP-84, along with other developmental items including a static test model. The contract was modified in June 1945 to incorporate the previous letter contract, which was now dropped. The aircraft suffered many development problems leading to a modified design being introduced in July 1945, with the third XP-84 to be built as the XP-84A.

The first of the XP-84's conducted its maiden flight from Muroc on 28 February 1946, followed by the second aircraft in August that year; both powered by the J35-GE-7 turbojet rated at 3,750 lb static thrust. The XP-84A, YP-84A and the initial production P-84 variant were powered by the Allison J35-A-15 rated at 4,000 lb static thrust.

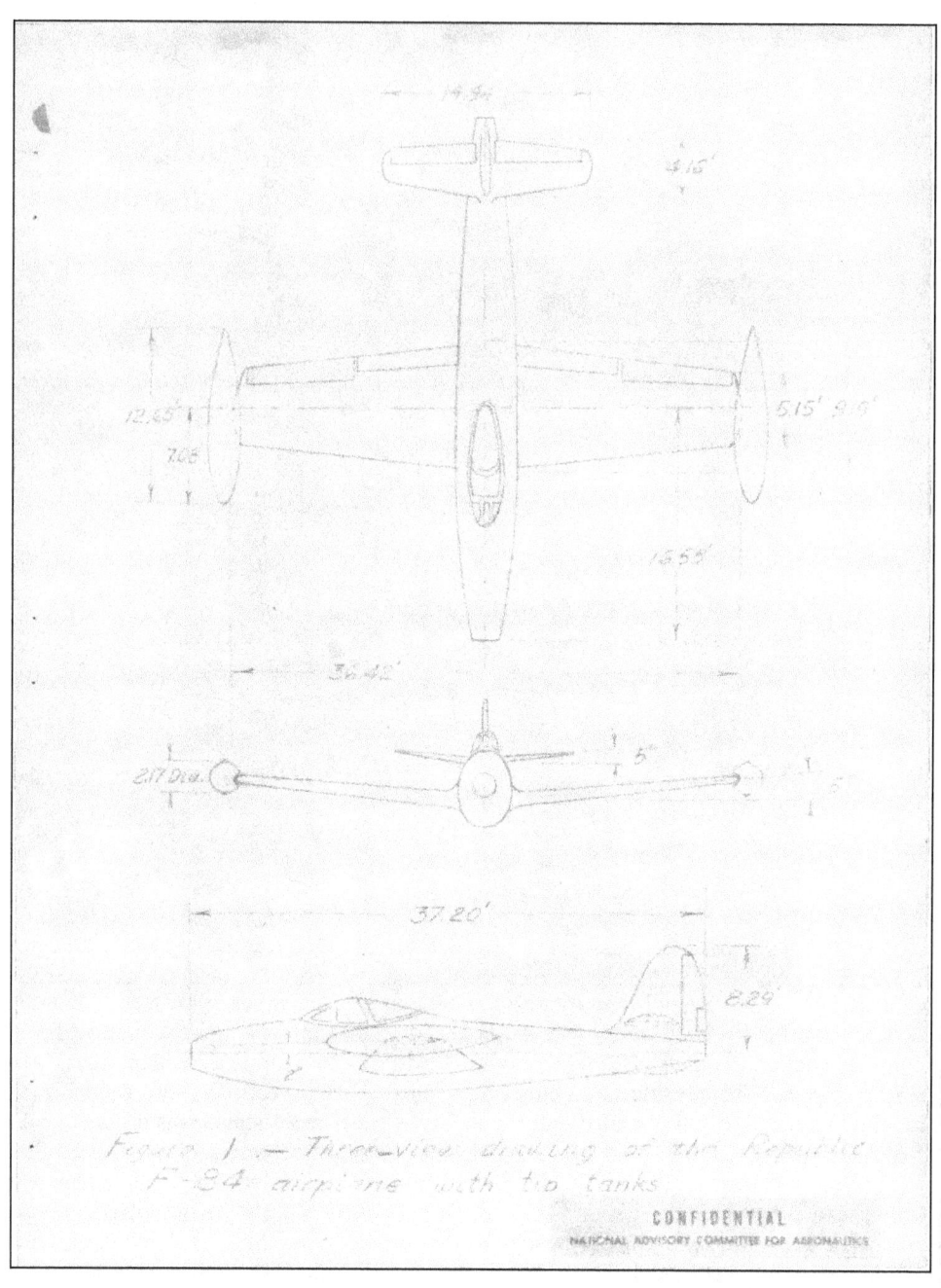

Previous page top: XP-84 S/N: 45-59475. USAF Previous page bottom: Three view of a one fifth scale model of the XP-84 fitted with a revised horizontal tail.

Above: This faint three-view general arrangement drawing of the Republic P-84 (F-84), showing the basic dimensions of the aircraft, comes from a 1940's test document. NASA Ames Research Centre

Top: XP-84 S/N: 45-59475. Above: The second XP-84, 45-59476, conducted its maiden flight in August 1946. AFFTC

The first of the XP-84's ordered took to the air for the first time on 26 February 1946, with second flying in August that year and an XP-84 was used to set a new US national speed record of 611-mph (983-km/h) in September 1946. Despite the speed record flight, the design suffered from weight problems and was underpowered, a problem which would effect a number of production variants.

The two XP-84s were followed by a single XP-84A and a batch of 15 YP-84A's (initially 25 YP-84's were planned), which were powered by the Allison J35-A-15 turbojet rated at 4,000-lb (8-kN) and used for USAAF service evaluation. The XP-84A had been completed more or less to YP-84A standard.

XP-84 S/N: 45-59475. USAF

Head-on view of an XP-84 showing the nose air intake for the J35 engine. USAF

The XP-84's were followed by a batch of YF-84A aircraft for service test. USAF

YP-84A S/N: 45-59495. USAF

YP-84A S/N: 45-59517. USAF

The YP-84A's were delivered to the USAAF in February 1947 for service evaluation. Unlike the XP-84's, these aircraft were armed with 6 x 0.50 in M2 machine guns; four in the upper forward fuselage area and two mounted in the wings. The YP-8A's were also equipped to carry wingtip drop tanks; the additional weight being compensated for by the more powerful engines. The P-84B, the first of which were delivered to the USAAF in summer 1947, was more or less an YP-84A armed with the M3 variant of the 0.50 in machine guns instead of the M2 in the YP-84A.

The P-84B (later F-84B) was the first production model of the Thunderjet. The PS- code was used when aircraft were designated 'P' for Pursuit, but was later changed to 'F' for fighter. USAF

P-84B 559561 at an air base in winter weather conditions. USAF

The P-84B attained an IOC (Initial Operational Capability) in December 1947 with the 14th Fighter Group based at Dow Field, Bangor, Maine. This IOC was, however, subject to a number of serious flying restrictions due to ongoing problems with the aircraft. The Ongoing structural problems with the P-84B saw the entire fleet grounded in May 1948 for inspection, after which aircraft were returned to flying status, albeit with many restrictions, while modifications were designed. In 1949, a program of structural modifications was introduced, including strengthening the wings and around 100 or so other structural enhancements. From the 86th P-84B, delivered in late 1947, the M3 machine gun armament was supplemented by eight rockets mounted in retractable launchers on the underside of the wings.

The last P-84B was delivered in June 1948, by which time 226 aircraft had been accepted; less than half of the aircraft ordered under various contracts. The balance of these contracts would be passed to later variants. The F-84B was phased out of the USAF inventory by the end of 1952.

An F-84B undergoing maintenance. USAF

The lack of fuselage space and thin wings meant that the F-84 could not carry much in the way of fuel internally; therefore, wingtip fuel tanks were fitted to production aircraft. The F-84B was equipped with an ejection seat and had provision for the carriage of rockets in the ground attack role. Other changes included introduction of the J35-A-15C engine, which was rated at the same 4,000-lb thrust as the -15 engine of the YP-84A.

A contract for the production of 99 P-84A's was cancelled in favour of production of the P-84B, which, therefore, became the first production variant with the first of 226 of this variant completed in June 1947. On 11 June 1948 the USAF changed the P (Pursuit) designation to F (Fighter) resulting in the P-84 being re-designated F-84.

The next production variant was the F-84C, 191 of which were delivered featuring some improvements over the F-84B including more reliable electrical system and the J35-A-13 engine rated at 4,000-lb (8-kN).

The F-84C was followed by the F-84D, 154 of which were built from F-84C contracts, introduced more radical changes including new wings, a longer fuselage, re-designed undercarriage and a more powerful J35-A-17D engine rated at 5,000-lb (10-kN) thrust, which was fed by a fuel system optimised for cold-weather.

The F-84E's, 843 built, incorporated a longer fuselage re-designed wingtip fuel tanks and a radar gun-sight. At least 100 of this variant were delivered to NATO air forces under the MSP (Mutual Security Program).

Although designed as a jet fighter, by the time of the Korean War in 1950 the F-84 was more at home as a first line fighter bomber, a role in which it was heavily employed by the USAF during that conflict. Thunderjet's were also involved in air combat operations, but were outclassed by PLAAF MiG-15.

Top and above: F-84C's. Note the aircraft at bottom is wearing 'P' for pursuit at the start of the 'buzz' code. USAF

The F-84C was basically an F-84B powered by a J35-A-13 engine and incorporating a new electrical system. A total of 191 F-84C's were delivered to the USAF, the first 11 going to the 20th Fighter Group in May 1948, with later deliveries going to the 33rd FG. The 31st and 78th FG's operated F-84C's along with F-84B's. The last F-84C was retired from active USAF service in 1952.

The F-84D retained the J35-A-13 engine (some records clearly show this variant as being powered by the -17D), but introduced a winterised fuel system, a thicker wing skin gauge and mechanical improvements to the undercarriage. The 1947 contract that led to the delivery of 191 F-84C was amended to cover delivery of an additional 154 aircraft designated F-84D, the first of which was delivered to the USAF in November 1948, with an additional 36 aircraft delivered before the end of the year and all 154 being delivered by the end of April 1949. The F-84D commenced its retirement from the active USAF inventory from late summer 1952, but served on with the ANG, which operated the 'D' until 1957.

An F-84D is seen in a climb over the Californian desert during the early 1950's. AFFTC

The F-84 was used primarily as a fighter-bomber in the Korean War. A major problem for the Thunderjet during its service career was its lack of engine thrust, resulting in the aircraft being underpowered, particularly when employed in the fighter-bomber role. The Thunderjet required a huge take-off roll even when carrying a modest bomb load, which saw the aircraft fly huge numbers of sorties, during the Korean War often with modest payloads.

To overcome the F-84's lack of performance, Republic embarked upon a swept wing variant, which emerged as the F-84F. However, the urgent need for more power and a larger load carrying capability led to the development of an interim variant

Top: A trio of F-84D's. USAF **Above: The USAF Flight Test Division operated this quartet of F-84's.** AFFTC

designated F-84G, which was basically an improved F-84D. This variant, was powered by a more powerful J35-A-29 turbojet engine rated at 5,600-lb thrust. While previous Thunderjet variants were most associated with conventional air to surface weapons such as rockets, bombs and napalm canisters, the F-84G was also tasked with theatre nuclear strike carrying a single free fall atomic weapon, the first USAF tactical fighter to be employed in this role. Indeed, tactical nuclear strike was the primary role for this variant, although it could also be used as a conventional fighter-bomber carrying up to 4,000-lb of ordnance. For operations with the free fall tactical nuclear bomb, the F-84G was equipped with a LABS (Low Altitude Bombing System).

USAF F-84E's. USAF

On 29 December 1948, the F-84 program was overhauled and a new contract provided for production of 409 F-84E's. The F-84E, powered by the J35-A-17 engine, introduced many changes including a lengthened fuselage, stronger wing, more spacious cockpit, a radar gun sight and improvements to the fuel system, which included the wingtip fuel tanks and provision for 230 US Gallon tanks under the wings, increasing the aircrafts combat radius to more than 1,000 miles.

The first production F-84E conducted its maiden flight on 18 May 1949 and was, along with another aircraft, accepted on the 26th of that month. Testing showed that the 'E' model was satisfactory in basic performance and maintainability, but problems arose with the A-1B sighting system leading to a suspension of deliveries until the A-1C sighting system became available in early 1950.

Various contracts saw 743 F-84E's delivered to the USAF and a further 100 delivered to MDAP customers; the last 3 aircraft being delivered in July 1951. The F-84E served with the USAF until 1956, at which time it was serving with TAC as a training aircraft. The Air Force Reserve relinquished its last F-84E's in 1957 and they were retired from ANG service in 1959.

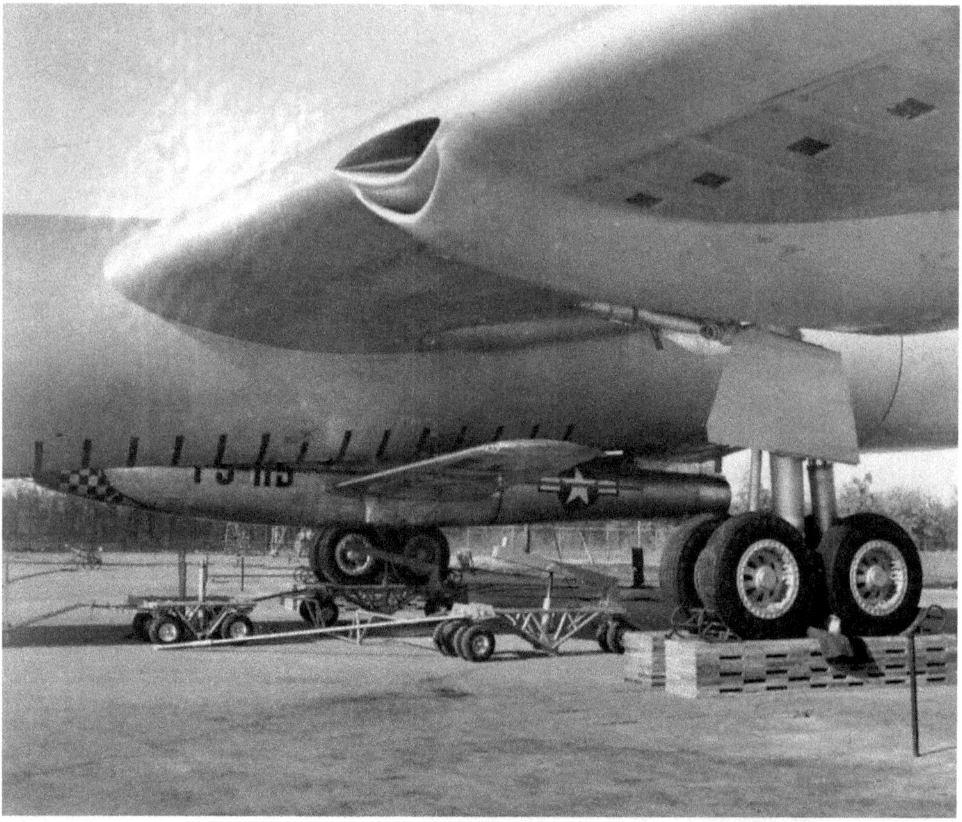

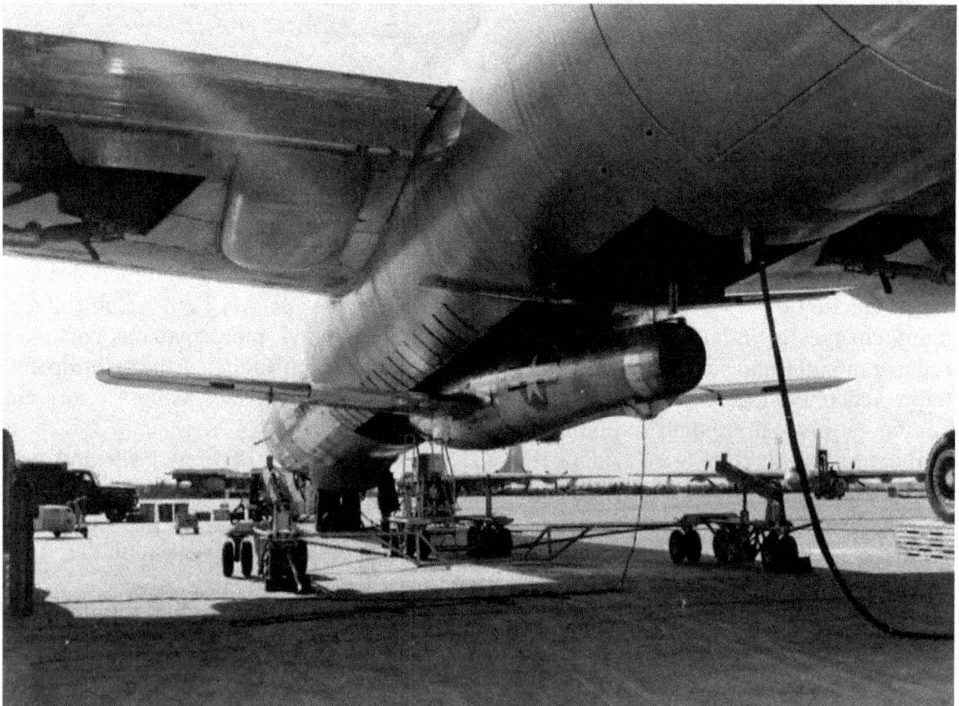

Previous page: The F-84E in the stowed position on the B-36. This page: The F-84E in the extended position (top) and retrieving position– long boom configuration (bottom). USAF

The F-84G, which was powered by an Allison J35-A-29, introduced a new in-flight refuelling system that allowed the aircraft to refuel from the new Boeing developed flying-boom refuelling system being adopted by SAC (he flying-boom compatible system did not appear on the F-84G until 1952). The 'G' featured an autopilot, A-4 gun sight (introduced from the 86th aircraft), a new ILS (introduced from the 301st aircraft) and could carry 4,000 lb of stores, with the capability to deliver atomic weapons (this capability was introduced in late 1951).

The first F-84G's were delivered in July 1951 and the aircraft entered service with SAC's 31st FEW (Fighter Escort Wing) based at Turner AFB, Georgia, which received its first aircraft in August 1951. A total of 3,025 F-84G's were accepted, with 789 of these entering service with the USAF and 2,236 (some documents suggest 1,936) going to MDAP recipients. The last production F-84G's, 21 MDAP aircraft were delivered in July 1953. By August 1954, SAC had retired the F-84G's, but it remained in service with TAC and the last aircraft was retired from USAF operational service in mid-1960.

Top: The F-84G was the most numerous variant of the Thunderjet built, with almost two-thirds of the 3,025 production aircraft built being delivered to NATO nations, and around 1,089 aircraft being delivered to the USAF. AFFTC

The F-84G was the first western tactical single-seat fighter to operate with tactical nuclear weapons, paving the way for future generations of supersonic nuclear armed strike fighters such as the F-100, F-101A/C and the F-105. The F-84G was equipped with an autopilot for long-range ferry flights, which were now part of operational doctrine courtesy of in-flight-refuelling.

Operational restrictions caused by the flying-boom in-flight refuelling method saw the F-84G equipped with the hose and drogue system developed across the Atlantic by Flight Refuelling in the United Kingdom. A pair of EF-84E's was converted in the UK and became the first jet powered fighter aircraft to cross the Atlantic non-stop courtesy of in-flight refuelling on 22 September 1950.

The F-84G was the most numerous variant of the Thunderjet with 3,025 aircraft built, 1,089 of which were delivered to the USAF.

Top: The ZELMAL (Zero Length Launch Mat) was an attempt to overcome the vulnerability of airfields to attack. AFFTC **Above: F-84 at the National Museum of the USAF.** USAF

In the early 1950's, the vulnerability of NATO airfields to attack, which might result in the denial of runways to aircraft, was considered serious and solutions to the problem were sought. One solution was inspired by early cruise missiles such as the Regulus and Matador, which were launched from small ramps in a manner not unlike that used by Germany with the V-1 Flying Bomb during World War II. Having amassed experience on the Matador ramp launched cruise missile program, the Glenn L Martin Company was awarded a contract to develop a system, which could be used in conjunction with the F-84G fighter-bomber.

The F-84G ZELMAL (Zero Length Launch Mat) program involved launching an F-84 from a zero length platform on a rocket booster, which propelled the F-84 to flying speed. The program, which was surprisingly straightforward, worked well with pilots on average suffering from no more stress during launch than that experience from a catapult launch from an aircraft carrier. The landing process proved to be more of a problem as the ZELMAL aircraft had its undercarriage removed to make launching easier. Instead of a conventional landing, the ZELMAL was equipped with an arrester hook, which would catch a wire and pull the fighter down onto a large portable air filled mat developed by Goodyear.

Phase I flight-testing began with the launch of an un-piloted EF-84G from a trailer mounted launcher at a remote spot on Rodgers Dry Lake on 15 December 1953. The first flight of the piloted F-84G ZELMAL was conducted on 5 January 1954. During the first landing of the ZELMAL F-84G the aircraft caught the arrestor wire, which pulled the aircraft down onto its belly on the runway. However, the aircraft skidded of the runway. The second piloted launch was conducted on 28 January 1954 and like the 5 January flight was brought down to a landing on a conventional runway with air mat landings not beginning until June that year. Although further landings worked better, support for the concept waned and the program was eventually cancelled.

A number of F-84 airframes were operated by NACA. The Langley Aeronautical Laboratory operated YF-84A S/N 45-59490 and the Ames Aeronautical Laboratory operated YF-84A S/N 45-59488. Both these aircraft were eventually transferred to the NACA HSFS (High Speed Flight Station) co-located at Muroc (later Edwards AFB) in November 1949 and December 1950 respectively. 45-59490 was used for some research flights and as a chase aircraft and pilot proficiency hack, while 45-59488 was used as a spares source for the first aircraft.

The US ANG operated large numbers of Thunderjet's with some 14 ANG squadrons receiving F-84B's before the start of the Korean War in June 1950. When additional aircraft were required for Korean service a number of ANG squadrons lost their F-84's, although nine other ANG squadrons converted to the Thunderjet during the Korean War period. Post Korean War, Thunderjet's were operated by 10 ANG squadrons with the last being retired in 1958.

When retired from operational service some F-84 airframes were used for test purposes and as target drones with 80 retired F-84B's converted as target drones for the USN.

Variants

XP-84: 3 prototype aircraft procured by the USAAF
YF-84A: 15 aircraft procured for service evaluation
F-84A: cancelled before any production
F-84B: 226 of this variant were delivered as the first production variant
F-84C: 191 aircraft delivered featuring some improvements over the F-84B
F-84D: 154 of this model were delivered featuring new wings and a longer fuselage.
F-84E: 843 F-84E's were delivered
F-84G: The most numerous variant with 3,025 aircraft produced. This variant was an improved F-84D and 1,936 of the 3,025 production examples were delivered to NATO nations under the MSP (Mutual Security Program)

F-84E

Engines: One Allison J35-A-17 rated at 4,900-lb thrust
Length: 38-ft 6-in
Height: 12-ft 7-in
Wingspan: 36-ft 5-in
Weights: 15,227-lb fully loaded
Maximum speed: 521 nautical miles per hour
Cruising speed: 485-mph
Service ceiling: 43,240-ft
Range: 1,485-miles

Top: In November 1950 the Fifth Air Force began receiving F-84's from the 27th FEG (Fighter Escort Group), the primary role of which was to protect Boeing B-29 Superfortress four engine bombers on daylight missions over North Korea. Outperformed by the more advanced MiG-15, the F-84 proved inadequate in the bomber escort role as would the Gloster Meteor F Mk.8 twin jet fighters of the Royal Australian Air Force's No.77 Squadron a year later. Here F-84s from the 27th FEG are being lifted onto the aircraft carrier *USS Bataan* for the journey across the pacific to Japan. Above: An F-84 during an engine change at Taegu airfield. USAF

Previous page top: The F-84 entered the Korean War in December 1950. Ground crew work on an F-84 in harsh winter conditions. F-84's of the 27th FEG. Outclassed in the air to air role by the Russian MiG-15, the F-84 would eventually be used primarily in the interdiction and close air support roles. In the ground attack role, the F-84 was a potent weapon armed with a variety of weapons. This aircraft is configured with 500 lb bombs and 5 in HVAR (High Velocity Aircraft Rockets). USAF

Top: F-84's were heavily utilised by the USAF during the Korean War, primarily in the ground attack role, but also participating in air combat operations. The Department of Defence reported 260 F-84's lost during this conflict. This four-ship of F-84's from the 474th FBW is en-route to a target north of the 38th Parallel in 1952. US DoD Above: An F-84 takes off for a mission over Korea carrying a very modest bomb-load. AFFTC

Top and centre: F-84's are prepared for ground armed with 500 lb bombs. Above: The air to air refuelling probe in the front of the starboard wingtip fuel tank of this F-84E was utilised under Operation High Tide to conduct long-range bombing missions against North Korean targets. USAF

Top on 16 May 1953, F-84E's attacked the Chosan irrigation dam. The first wave of 24 aircraft attained underwater hits, causing a 'tidal wave' of water to pour over the spillway. A second wave of F-84E's then attacked, achieving 'direct hit in a concentrated area, causing a breach in the eastern wall of the dam. Above: Under the code name Operation High Tide, aerial refuelled missions involving F-84's flying non-stop from Japan to bomb targets in North Korea commenced in May 1952. When 12 F-84E's flew from Japan and bombed targets in North Korea refuelled by KB-29 tanker aircraft. USAF

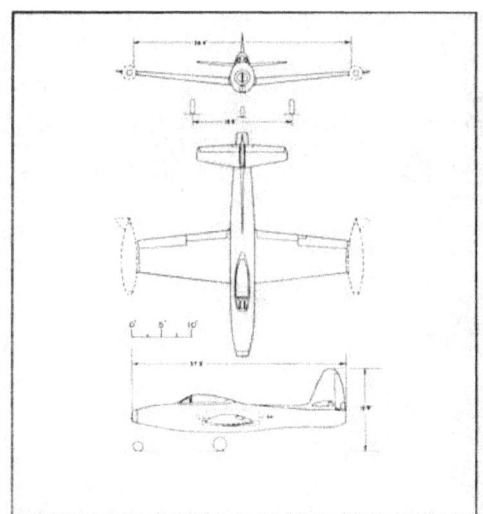
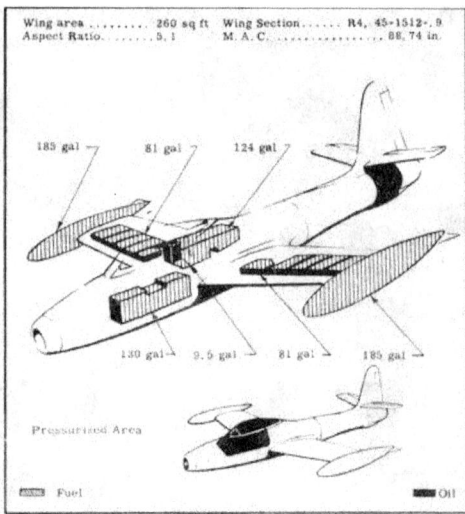
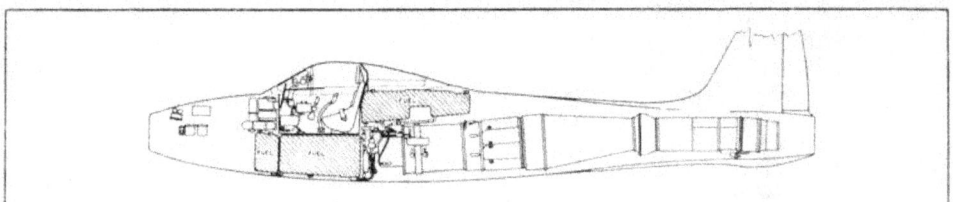

F-84B 9 January 1950. USAF

F-84D/E's were deployed to Korea in December 1950, serving with the 27th FEW (Fighter Escort Wing). Due to substantial losses in fighter bombers, particularly during the railway interdiction campaign, combined with normal operational losses, Fifth Air Force began to receive additional F-84D's in spring 1952; 102 aircraft, most of which were allocated to the 136th Wing, which was a former ANG unit. Despite these reinforcements the F-84D was withdrawal from operational service as new variants began to appear in numbers in August and September 1952. The F-84E's inability to adequately protect the Boeing B-29 Bombers led to its gradual withdrawal from the bomber escort role; however, it performed adequately in the new role of ground attack and interdiction.

The F-84E, like previous models, despite being rated satisfactory in regards to maintenance, was plagued with operational problems, which at times were so acute that something in the order of 50% of the USAF F-84 inventory was non-serviceable. An example of this is the fact that of the 60 F-84E's deployed to the FEAF in December 1950, only 27 aircraft were actually fully operational capable.

The F-84G began to equip units of the Fifth Air Force in the Far East during summer 1952, with increasing numbers becoming available by September that year. The 9th FBS of the 49th Wing was transferred from Korea to Japan in December 1952 to allow the crews to be trained in the delivery of tactical atomic bombs.

The in-flight refuelling capability of the F-84G was used operationally during the later stages of the Korean War. In March 1953, F-84G's attacked the industrial centre at Chonjin located on North Korea's east coast some 40 miles south of the Manchurian North Korean border.

During the Korean War Fifth Air Force lost 335 F-84D/E/G's, the majority of which were brought down by ground fire ranging from small arms to anti-aircraft guns.

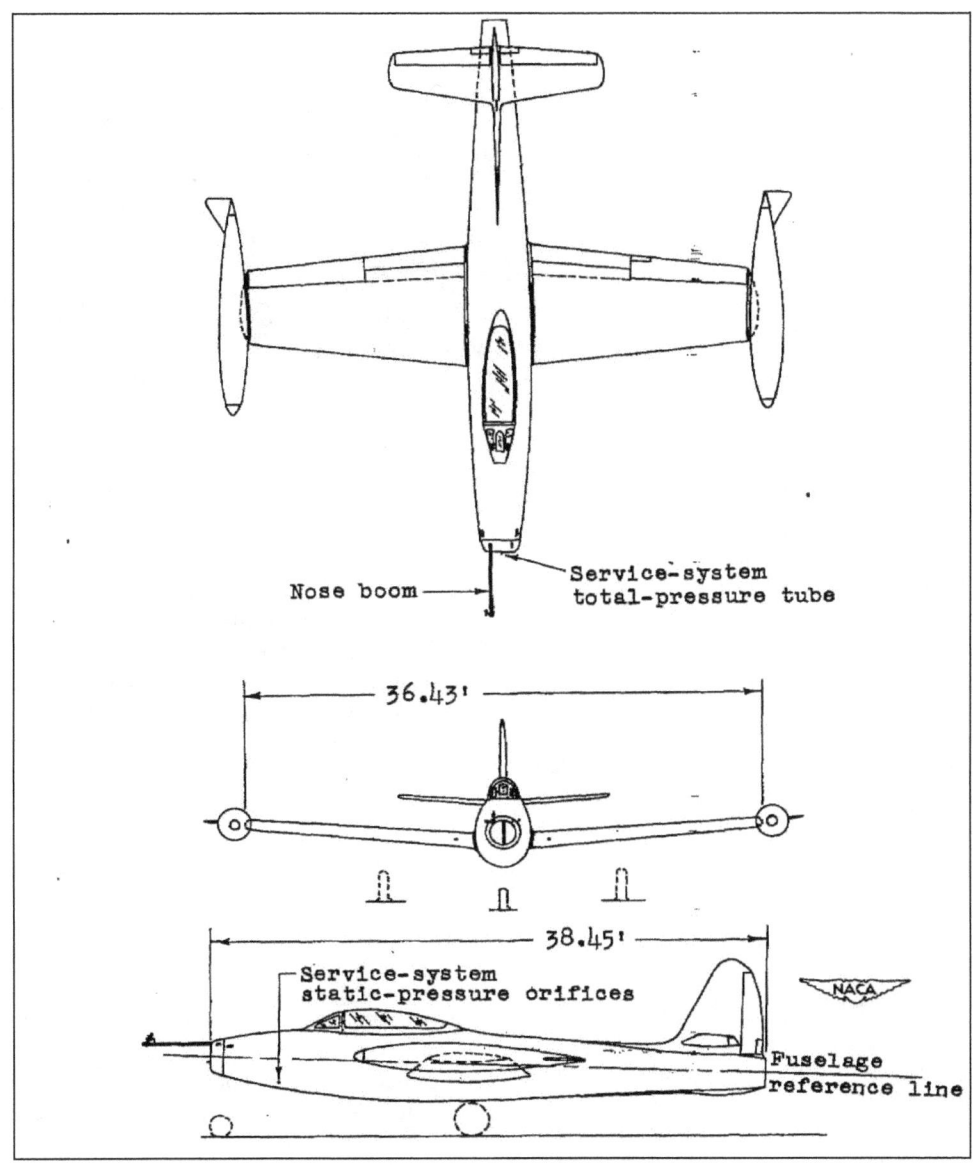

Three-view general arrangement drawing of an F-84G aircraft with test instrumentation fitted for Squadron Operational Training. NACA/NASA

Republic F-84F Thunderstreak

The XF-84F prototype S/N: 49-2430 was initially ordered under the designation YF-96A. AFFTC

Concerns about the lack of performance of the straight wing F-84 compared with fighters such as the North American F-86 Sabre led Republic, in 1949, to embark upon a program to dramatically improve performance of the straight wing F-84, which led to the F-84F Thunderstreak featuring a 40 degrees sweptback wing at 25% of the chord. Although retaining around 60% commonality with the straight wing F-84 the new aircraft would emerge as a quite different aircraft with increased capabilities and dramatically improved performance over its forebear. Much of the fuselage remained common with the first generation F-84, however, a number of significant design changes were introduced such as replacing the heavily framed bubble canopy of the Thunderjet, which slid back to open, with a more streamlined upwards-hinging canopy. The F-84F and derivatives also relinquished the anti-glare panel on the rear fuselage and had grid style perforated air brakes, which were located on the fuselage sides just aft of the wing trailing edge.

The production F-84F featured a solid turtleback with dark rear-view panels, which were generally considered to be of little use. The new tail plane unit adopted was a one-piece stabilator, then known as a flying tail, which was beginning to replace the traditional elevator controls. A taller swept-back vertical tail replaced the short rounded vertical tail found on the first generation F-84. The tail section could be removed for engine changes and maintenance. The small wingtip fuel tanks of the first generation F-84 were replaced by comparatively large external tanks carried beneath the wings.

Initially the Thunderstreak was to be designated F-96 with a single prototype YF-96A S/N: 49-2430 being ordered. This aircraft, which was built from an F-84E, was re-designated XF-84F when the Thunderstreak was re-designated F-84F. The prototype XF-84F flew for the first time on 3 June 1950 (the AFFTC states that first flight took place on 14

Top: The first production F-84F-1-RE S/N: 51-1346 during a test flight. USAF
Above: The wingtip tanks of the Thunderjet were omitted from the F-84F, which could carry a pair of large external fuel tanks below the inner wings. AFFTC

February 1951) powered by a J35-A-25 turbojet producing 5,200-lb (10.5-kN) thrust. Performance with this engine was inadequate, therefore, the first prototype was used in an experimental program in an attempt to solve the problem of poor climb performance, which was considered to be sluggish, a problem which had bedevilled the first generation straight wing F-84 and remained a problem with the XF-84F. The aircraft was fitted with a British Rolls Royce Sapphire turbojet, which necessitated deepening of the fuselage with an elliptical nose air intake. This engine improved performance of the aircraft and two further XF-84F's were built featuring a larger fuselage and the Wright J65 turbojet engine (which was basically a licence produced Rolls

Top: F-84F-5-RE S/N: 51-1366. Above: F-84F-20-RE S/N: 51-1443 takes on fuel from Boeing KB-29 tanker aircraft S/N: 44-83922. USAF

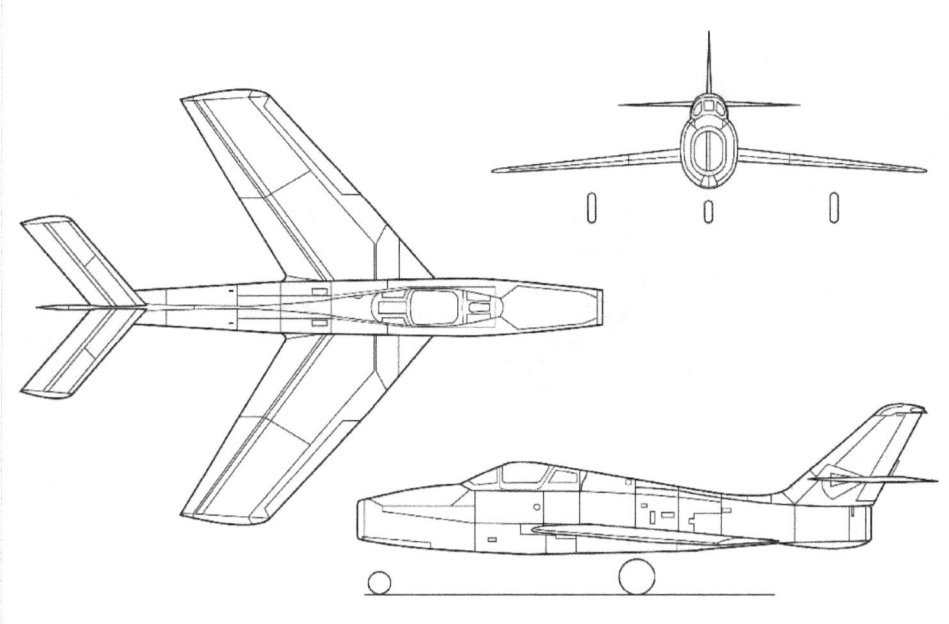

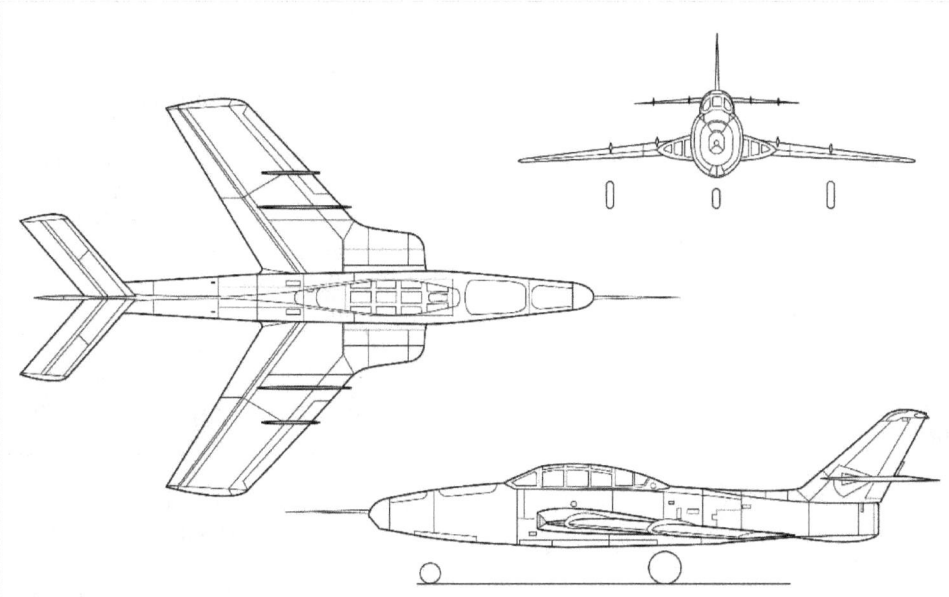

Top: General arrangement 3-view drawing of the F-84F shows the departure from the straight wing design of its forebear in favour of the swept-back wing. Much of the F-84 Thunderjet remained, although in appearance the F-84F appeared more or less a new design. Above: General arrangement 3-view drawing of the YRF-84F prototype of the tactical reconnaissance variant of the F-84F. This variant relinquished the characteristic nose air intake in favour of two smaller wing-root mounted intakes leaving the nose free to house a camera suite. Both NASA

The XF-84F was delivered to Edwards AFB in May 1950 and Phase I flight testing by a Republic Test pilot commenced in June that year, lasting around one month. The Phase II testing, flown by USAF test pilots, was completed during November 1950 with 65 flights conducted in around 70 flight hours. The XF-84F had been powered by a J35-A-25 engine rated at 5,300 lb static thrust, which was shown to be completely inadequate if the aircraft was to conduct the missions it was designed for.

It was hoped to overcome the aircraft's poor performance by replacing the J35 with the YJ65, which was basically a British Armstrong-Siddely Sapphire turbojet engine, built under licence by the Curtiss-Wright Corporation. This engine had been selected as the most suitable for a production F-84F. In November 1950, AMC (Air Material Command) had suggested that two more development aircraft be built; this time powered by the Sapphire (YJ65) engine in order that this combination could be tested before any production decision was made. However, in December the USAF ordered the aircraft to go forward to production before the new prototypes had flown.

The first of these new XF-84F (sometimes referred to as YF-84F) prototypes conducted its maiden flight from the AFFTC at Edwards on 14 February 1951. This aircraft, which was powered by a standard British manufactured Sapphire engine, had a good overall performance, but was considered unsafe resulting in flying restrictions being imposed.

Top: An F-84F Thunderstreak conducts a JATO (Jet Assisted Take-Off) carrying a load of air to ground rockets. JATO went some way to solving the problem of long take-off run which had plagued the first generation F-84 and remained a problem with the F-84F. AFFTC

Royce Sapphire. The first few hundred F-84F's delivered were powered by J65-W-1 or -1A engines with the remainder of the 2,711 aircraft produced powered by the more powerful J65-W-3 turbojet rated at 7,220-lb (14.6-kN) with afterburner.

Deliveries of the F-84F commenced to the USAF TAC (Tactical Air Command) in 1954 with the aircraft's primary role being an air to ground support fighter-bomber. A total of 2,711 F-84F's were produced – 2,112 by Republic and 599 by General Motors. More than half of this total - 1,301 - was delivered to NATO nations.

From the side-on aspect the F-84F's Thunderjet lineage was apparent, particularly the chubby forward fuselage. AFFTC

A tactical reconnaissance variant of the F-84F was developed designated RF-84F Thunderflash of which 715 were built including 386 delivered to NATO nations. Two F-84F's were converted on the production line to YRF-84F standard, which involved fitting a pair of short air intakes at the wing roots, which left the long solid nose section free to house a suite of cameras for the photographic reconnaissance role. The new intake design had the drawback of reducing overall thrust for the engine, with the knock on effect of reduced performance, with the speed of the Thunderflash being no faster than the F-84F, despite the higher power of the J65-W-7 turbojet rated at 7,800-lb (15.7-kN) thrust with afterburner.

The RF-84F was claimed as the first reconnaissance aircraft to be equipped with a suite of standard aerial cameras and a dicing camera for close-up images of points of interest. It was also the first reconnaissance tactical fighter type aircraft to be equipped with a Tri-Metragon camera, which was used for horizon-to-horizon work and a camera control system and a viewfinder in the cockpit, which could be viewed by the pilot, who also doubled as the photographer.

The YRF-84F with S/N: 51-1826 was first flown in February 1952 with the successful flight testing leading to a production run of 715 RF-84F's

Front instrument cockpit panel of an F-84F. USAF

The YRF-84F (background) was the prototype for the tactical reconnaissance variant of the F-84F, later receiving the name Thunderflash. AFFTC

F-84F's served in USAF first line units as tactical fighter bombers armed with conventional stores and as tactical nuclear strike fighters armed with a single tactical free fall nuclear weapon until replacement by more modern aircraft like the North American F-100 Super Sabre in the late 1950's when the aircraft were handed over to US ANG units. A number of F-84F's were temporarily recalled into USAF active service at the time of the Berlin crisis in the early 1960's. F-84F's equipped 24 ANG squadrons from 1955 until the last was withdrawn in 1972. The RF-84F was operated by 11 ANG squadrons from 1956 until the last was retired in 1972. Another two ANG squadrons temporarily operated RF-84F's between 1962 and 1964, while F-84F's had been taken over by USAF active duty squadrons.

Although the USAF had cancelled the McDonnell XF-85 Goblin parasite fighter program in the late 1940's, SAC (Strategic Air Command) was still extremely worried about the vulnerability of its fleet of huge lumbering Convair B-36 Peacemaker strategic bombers to enemy defensive interceptors. The parasite fighter concept had not died with the XF-85 program, however, and a number of solutions were looked at using more conventional fighters, which would have better performance than the XF-85, which was limited by the constraints of its extremely small size. Republic converted one of the early prototype YF-84F's with downward pointing (anhedral or cathedral) horizontal stabilisers to allow it to clear the fuselage of the B-36 bomber mother ship. A retractable nose-hook was fitted to enable the aircraft to be recovered in flight. Once converted' the aircraft was known as the YF-84F FICON (Fighter Conveyor). Testing showed that the basic FICON principal was feasible, however, the full size fighter hung under the fuselage of the B-36 had only

Top: RF-84F-5-RE S/N: 51-1844. Above: The RF-84F was conceived as a replacement for the RF-80, which proved to be inadequate during operations in Korea. USAF

The Thunderflash was produced in two main variants, the standard RF-84F (top) and the RF-84F FICON (above). The latter variant was a standard RF-84F equipped to be air launched from a Convair GRB-36 Peacemaker mother ship. Both AFFTC

a few inches of clearance from the runway when carrying under wing fuel tanks. Furthermore, the drag of the B-36 bomber increased considerably when carrying a fighter hung beneath the fuselage reducing speed and increasing vulnerability and the same problems of launch and recovery when under attack by enemy fighters that existed with the XF-85 program remained with the FICON program.

Then YF-84F FICON was an attempt to produce a parasite escort fighter, which could be launched from Convair B-36 strategic bombers. AFFTC

The parasite program was dropped in so far as providing fighter escort to the B-36 was concerned. However, by the mid-1950's, the B-36 was being replaced in service by the slightly smaller, but faster and less vulnerable jet powered Boeing B-52 Stratafortress strategic bomber. The B-36, however still formed a large part of SAC's fleet and the FICON concept was looked at again to fill a reconnaissance role. The huge RB-36 strategic reconnaissance aircraft were extremely vulnerable to ground and air defences, particularly over target areas. The FICON program was refined to mate an RF-84F Thunderflash with the huge RB-36, which would release the Thunderflash at a set distance from the reconnaissance target allowing the less vulnerable Thunderflash to photograph the target area before returning to the mothership to be recovered in-flight for the journey back to base.

Despite problems of poor ground clearance and increased drag, which led to the cancellation of the F-84F FICON program, remaining, the RF-84F/RB-36 hybrid program progressed and around 25 aircraft were converted allowing a full squadron to be established for use in the strategic reconnaissance role, although these saw only very brief service. Designations of GRF-84F and F-84K have been associated with these aircraft, although they were generally referred to in the USAF as RF-84F Thunderflash.

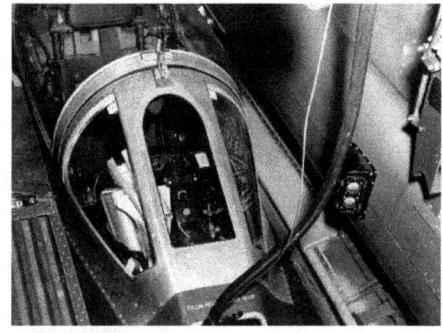

The YF-84F FICON cockpit with the aircraft in the stowed position beneath the mother ship. The YF-84F FICON was not a success and the program was abandoned together with the parasite escort fighter concept. USAF

An RF-84F hooks-up to the mother ship. USAF

On 9 April 1951, the USAF issued a contract for the production of 274 F-84F's. Over the course of the next year a number of contract supplements raised production contracts to 719 aircraft. Republic had contracted to deliver the first F-84F production aircraft in December 1951, but this did not take place until November 1952 and the USAF took delivery of two F-84F's on 3 December that year. The first 274 F-84F's were powered by the YJ65-W-1 engine, while later aircraft were powered by the YJ65-W-1A and -W-3 engines.

The F-84F entered operational service with SAC 506th Strategic Fighter Wing based at Dow AFB, Maine in January 1954. However, the aircraft were subjected to many restrictions, being of limited operational use. This would apply to the several hundred early production F-84F's powered by the YJ65-W-1 and W-1A engines. The J65 powered aircraft achieved initial operational capability on 12 May 1954 with aircraft delivered to TAC's 405th FBW at Langley, AFB, Virginia. SAC's J65 powered aircraft entered service with the 27th SFW (Strategic Fighter Wing) at Bergstrom AFB on 18 June 1954.

The F-84F program continued to bedevilled by problems resulting in production suspensions and groundings, then accelerated production. Eventually a total of 2,348 F-84F's were delivered, 1,496 for the USAF and 852 for MAP, with the last Republic built aircraft, for MAP, being delivered in August 1957. The last Republic built F-84F for the USAF had been delivered in February 1957, with the last General Motors delivered F-84F being delivered in February 1955. The delivery totals for the USAF were 756 lower than originally planned. In addition to the production aircraft Republic also delivered the 3 XF/YF-84F's for testing.

In January 1958 the last F-84F's were retired from TAC, SAC having turned its aircraft over to the ANG some time before. However, TAC was equipped with a number of F-84F's in July 1958 for training purposes with ATC. Four ANG F-84F Wings were brought to active service during the Berlin Crisis of October 1961. Other ANG F-84F's went to TAC for training and when the crisis abated, the USAF retained a number of the aircraft to equip newly activated TAC units pending re-equipment with more modern aircraft. However, the 222 aircraft used to equip these units, the 12th and 15th and 366th TFW's, were increasingly maintenance heavy resulting in groundings. The final phase out of active USAF service occurred in July 1964, when TAC returned the last aircraft to the ANG, which retired its last aircraft in 1972.

Top and centre: The YF-84F FICON. Note the nose mounted apparatus for hooking up to the grab mechanism on the Convair B-36 Mother ship. Above: The YF-84H. Note the redesigned 'T' tail. USAF

The F-84H was a re-design of the F-84F to accommodate a massive turboprop engine with a propeller designed to attempt to achieve supersonic speeds. AFFTC

Republic converted two F-84F airframes to XF-84H standard to be used as test bed aircraft for development of a high performance turboprop fighter aircraft. The conversion was so extensive that the XF-84H's emerged as virtually new aircraft powered by a single 5,332-hp (horse power) Allison XT-40-A-1 turboprop engine with a heavy drive shaft, which led to a gearbox that was responsible for rotating the huge three bladed propellers at supersonic speeds. The supersonic propeller design was the result of collaboration between the Wright Air Development Centre, Hamilton Strand and Curtiss-Wright. The performance of conventional propellers was found to be eroded significantly as the tips approached supersonic speeds, which effectively put a limit on the achievable speeds of propeller driven fighter aircraft. The new design was aimed at achieving supersonic speeds.

To make room for the propeller the characteristic F-84 nose air intake was deleted and two smaller intakes positioned at the wing roots with the left intake positioned about 1-ft forward of the right intake as part of the efforts to reduce the torresion effects of the propeller. While the tail horizontal stabilisers were set about a third way up the vertical tail on the F-84F, the XF-84H's were fitted with a horizontal stabiliser set almost at the top of the vertical tail. This was required to lift the horizontal stabilisers above the ferocious twisting airflow from the propeller. A small triangular fin was fitted to the dorsal spine just aft of the cockpit to help reduce torsion flow and a small emergency ram air turbine was located just ahead of the fin. Differential control of the wing flaps was incorporated, which were in effect the first use of flaperons. Before settling on the three-bladed propeller, a number of designs were tested including a six-bladed contra-rotating small-diameter airscrew.

Although the program was aimed at producing a turboprop fighter capable of supersonic speed, the aircraft proved disappointing in this respect, reaching a speed of only 520-mph, which fell far short of the initially planed 670-mph. The 520-mph speed has been reported as being the fastest speed ever achieved by a propeller driven aircraft, however, this appears not to be the case as the Soviet Union had flown the Tu-95

Top: The first of two XF-84H's was flown for the first time on 22 July 1955. However, the program proved to be disappointing from a performance aspect leading to cancellation. AFFTC Above: The second of the two XF-84H's. USAF

'Bear' intercontinental strategic bomber aircraft which is now accepted as having had a maximum speed of around 570-575-mph. More of a problem than the lack of performance was the immense howling noise generated by the powerful engine, which caused detrimental effects on pilots and ground crew with many people suffering ill effects on coming into contact with the effects of the engine. The unacceptably heavy screeching noise was caused by heavy subliminal vibrations, which led directly to the aircraft being nicknamed the Thunderscreech.

The first of 2 XF-84H's conducted its maiden flight at Edwards AFB on 22 July 1955. However, the program was soon cancelled as the supersonic turboprop fighter was proving to be unattainable and impractical and the USAF and USN were firmly focussed on procuring conventional jet powered fighter designs.

The YF-84J was an attempt to wring out additional performance from the F-84F. Two F-84F's were converted on the production line to YF-84J standard, which was developed as a simple upgrade from the F-84F. Main changes from the F-84F included a new engine in the shape of the General Electric XJ73-GE-5 turbojet, which produced 2,000 lb more thrust over the F-84F's power plant. Fitment of the new engine required small changes to the airframe

The YF-84J was developed as a simple upgrade of the F-84F in an attempt to gain additional performance from the design. Two YF-84J's were built as conversions from F-84F's on the production line. AFFTC

including a slight deepening of the fuselage and an increased area oval air intake to increase airflow to the engine.

The YF-84J was delivered to Edwards AFB on 24 April 1954 and during testing the performance was considered to be acceptable, however, maintenance of this variant was more problematic than the F-84F, which led to the decision not to go-ahead with production or conversions of service F-84F's. During flight testing the YF-84J apparently attained a speed of Mach 1.09 on 7 May 1954. The second YF-85J was cancelled before it flew.

The RF-84K designation was applied to RF-84F's converted for operations from GRB-36 Peacemaker, a sideline of the FICON program.

A number of Thunderstreak and Thunderflash's were used in trials and test programs with various service branches and other agencies. The NACA HSFS acquired the sole YRF-84F S/N: 51-1828 in April 1954 and used the aircraft for research flights and as a chase aircraft supporting other research programs. NACA also operated YF-84F S/N: 49-2430 on loan from the USAF, which was used to study the effectiveness of aircraft ailerons prior to spoilers being incorporated.

XF-84F: A single aircraft converted from an F-84E with swept-back wings and tail developed as the YF-96A

XF-84F: Two further prototypes powered by a Wright J65 turbojet engine and built with an enlarged fuselage. Also referred to as YF-84F

F-84F: 2,711 production swept-wing fighters

YRF-84F: 1 prototype photographic reconnaissance variant of the F-84F fighter S/N: 51-1826

RF-84F: 715 production tactical reconnaissance fighters

RF-84K Thunderflash. USAF

The first YRF-84F flew in February 1952 and the first production standard RF-84F flew on 9 September 1953. The RF-84F entered service with TAC in March 1954 and SAC in December 1955, when SAC equipped a SRW (Strategic Reconnaissance Wing) with a mix of RF-84F and RF-84K's. (The RF-84K was developed for deployment from the GRB-36 Reconnaissance/Bomber under the FICON program). While early RF-84F's were powered by the -3 engine later production was powered by the -7 rated at 7,800 lb. Although it was initially equipped for the fixed boom refuelling system the RF-84F received modifications allowing it to use the probe and drogue refuelling system.

A total of 715 RF-84F's were delivered, 388 for the USAF and 327 going to MAP customers. 25 of the USAF RF-84F's were modified to RF-84K standard. Production ended with delivery of the last 29 MAP aircraft in December 1957.

The 71st SRW's last RF-84F/K mission was flown on 22 May 1957, following which the aircraft was gradually retired with the last aircraft being handed over the ANG in 1958. The aircraft was retired from ANG service on 26 January 1972 when the last aircraft were flown into storage.

F-84F
Engines: One Wright (Rolls Royce Sapphire) J65-W-3 turbojet rated at 7,220-lb thrust
Length: 43-ft 5-in
Height: 15-ft
Wingspan: 33-ft 7-in
Weights: 27,000-lb maximum take-off
Maximum speed: 685-mph – 35,000 ft
Cruising speed: 535-mph
Service ceiling: 44,450-ft
Range: 1,900-miles
Armament: six x 0.5-in heavy machine guns and 24 x 5-in unguided rockets or 6,000-lb of bombs
Crew: One

RF-84F
Engines: One Wright (Rolls Royce Sapphire) J65-W-7 turbojet rated at 7,800-lb thrust
Length: 47-ft 6-in
Height: 15-ft
Wingspan: 33-ft 6-in
Weights: 25,390-lb maximum take-off
Maximum speed: 629-mph
Cruising speed: 542-mph
Service ceiling: 39,390-ft
Range: 2,000-miles
Armament: four x wing-mounted 0.5-in heavy machine guns
Crew: One

McDonnell XF-85 Goblin

The portly appearance of the XF-85 was necessitated by the requirement to keep the aircraft as small as possible to fit the confines of the Convair B-36 bomb bay. USAF

The McDonnell XF-85 Goblin was an unsuccessful attempt to produce a parasite fighter, which could be carried in the capacious bomb bay of the large Convair B-36 Peacemaker strategic bomber. The fighter would then be launched to defend the bomber from enemy air defence fighters. The sheer size of the B-36, combined with the fact that it was equipped with four bomb bays, meant that the large bomber could still carry a huge offensive payload as well as a parasite escort fighter. Once any engagement was over the parasite fighter would be recovered in flight assuming it and the mother ship bomber had survived. Of course all of this was theoretical and assumed that the enemy interceptors would oblige by not engaging the B-36 while it was in the extremely vulnerable position of going through the complex launch procedure and even more complex recovery, which would require the bomber to slow down and hold a steady course vastly increasing its vulnerability. Weather would also be a factor.

The idea of Parasite fighters was not new. A number of programs were tested in the years before World War II, including an ambitious program in the Soviet Union in the 1930's, with varying degrees of success. However, it was felt that this type of operation would be unpractical in an operational environment and was therefore dropped by the Soviets.

The impracticality and vulnerability of the Parasite fighter concept appeared to be lost on the USAAF in the late stages of World War II and the years immediately following the war's end. Another sticking point for the Parasite fighter concept was the vulnerability of the Parasite fighter itself, which due to size and weight limitations was never going to be able to compete on a level playing field with conventional fighters of the day.

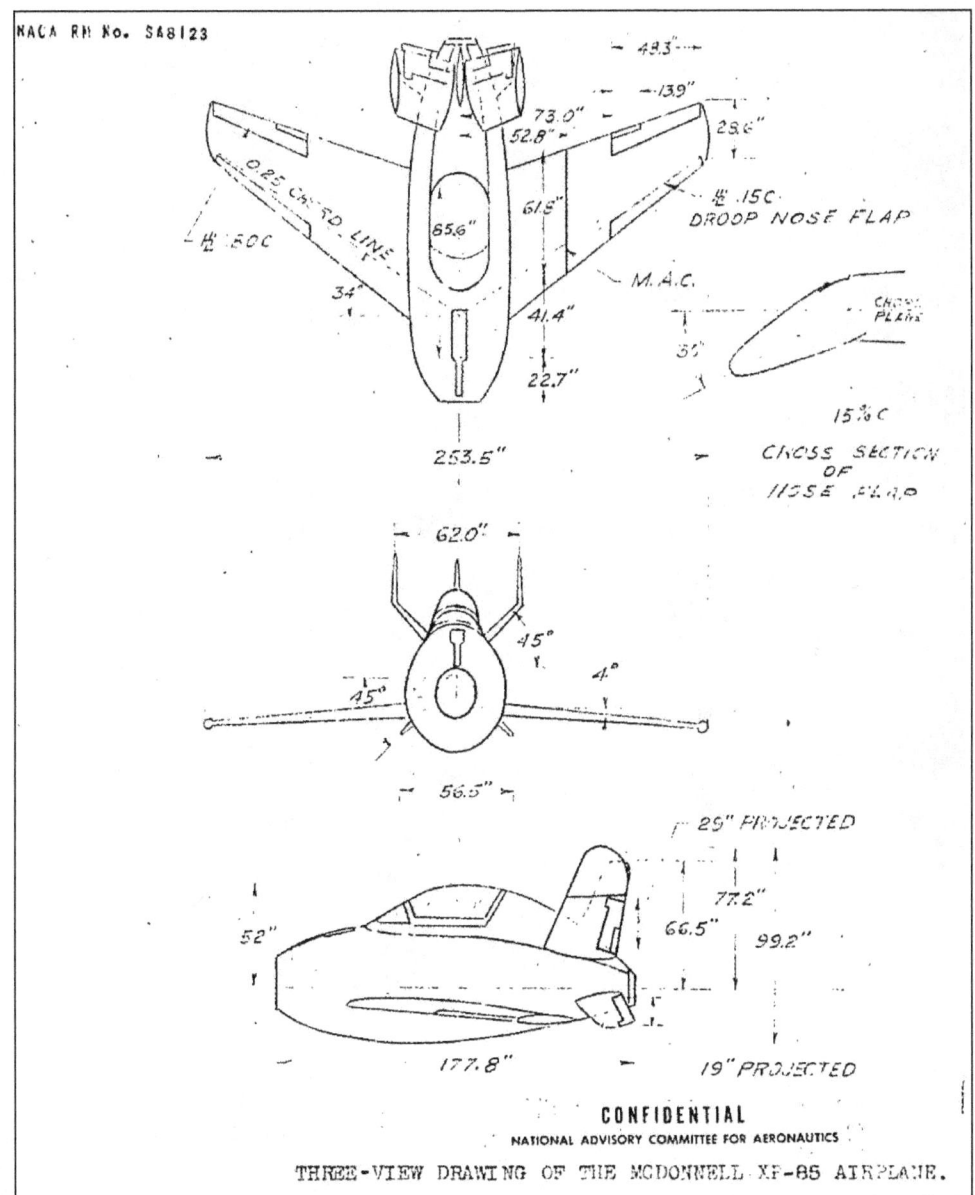

General arrangement drawing of the XP-85 studied by NACA shows the general layout of the full size aircraft. NASA

Undeterred by the negatives of the Parasite fighter concept the USAAF embarked upon the XP-85 program with a sort of enthusiasm. When required, the plan was for the XP-85 (or an operational P-85) to be lowered on a trapeze from the B-36 bomb bay and be released. A number of tests were conducted with the system on a Boeing EB-29B Superfortress bomber. However, the impracticalities of the aircraft, by then re-designated XF-85, combined with the slowly maturing technology for in-flight refuelling, led to the programs cancellation without the XF-85 ever being carried aloft and released by a B-36.

Top: An XP-85 in the NASA Ames 40 x 80 ft wind tunnel during Force and Moment Tests. NASA

A specially constructed loading pit was built for the XP-85 program. The loading procedure involved the XP-85 being housed in the pit and the bomber reversed over before the aircraft was lifted into the bomb bay. AFFTC

Previous page: The XP-85 is shown in the stowed position with the wings folded (top) and in the lowered position with wings extended for launching (bottom). This page: These views of the XP-85 show just how small the aircraft was. USAF

The XP-85's small size limited the size and power of the engines, armament and operational equipment, which all had to be kept to the bare minimum. USAF

In the days and months following the end of World War II the USAAF issued requirement MX-472, which called for a parasite fighter. The traditional US fighter manufacturers showed a complete lack of interest, however, the relatively new company of McDonnell Aircraft seized the parasite fighter proposal as its chance to try and break into the wholesale fighter manufacturing business for the USAAF. McDonnell had previously built the XP-67 twin piston engine fighter, which did not go into production, and was working on the FH-1 Phantom jet carrier borne fighter for the USN. However, the company took on the parasite fighter program on the understanding that it would also receive a contract for conventional fighters in the shape of the XP-88 Voodoo penetration fighter.

The XP-85 was eventually named Goblin, which, along with the Phantom appellate applied to the McDonnell FH-1 carrier capable naval jet fighter being developed at the same time, began the long association of ghostly and supernatural names for its jet fighters.

The new parasite fighter was to be powered by a single non-afterburning Westinghouse XXXJ35 turbojet rated at 3,000-lb. The aircrafts small size – only just over 14-ft long (dictated by the constraints of the B-36 bomb bays required to house the aircraft) meant that there was little room for installation of the engine and systems. Space limitations also meant that the aircraft would have to forgo the luxury of air interception radar, effectively limiting the fighter to daylight operations, a major handicap since the B-36 was a truly intercontinental bomber capable of flying missions well in excess of 24-hours.

With the XF-85 carried beneath the bomb bay, the EB-29 Mother ship, 'Monstro', S/N: 44-8411, thunders down the runway at Muroc during the test program. AFFTC

The cramped conditions meant that the pilot sat in a cockpit atop the engine with a relatively light planned armament of four 0.5-in heavy machine guns mounted in the upper nose - 2 each side of the open nose air intake. No armament was ever fitted to the XF-85's. The requirement called for the aircraft to carry sufficient fuel for a one-hour flight and have a reasonable degree of manoeuvrability and a design maximum speed theoretically put at 650-mph. Such performance was always going to be a problem in an aircraft with the dimensions of the XF-85, which included folding wings of 21-ft span.

McDonnell built 2 XF-85's and the first free flight took place on 23 August 1948. From the very beginning it became apparent that the practicality of the design was stretching the limits. Among the main problems was instability caused by the short stubby fuselage. The aircraft was eventually fitted with six tail fins, which were canted at a variety of angles, but these simply failed to provide adequate keel area resulting in winglets being fitted to the wingtips. However, these fixes failed to solve the problem, resulting in major problems being encountered during mid-air launch and recovery procedures.

The EB-29B Superfortress used for tests with the XF-85 received the name 'Monstro' after the Whale in Carlo Collodi's 1883 children's Novel 'The Adventures of Pinocchio'. The loading process involved the XF-85 being placed into a deep loading pit then the EB-29 would be towed over the pit, the trapeze extended and the XF-85 hooked up and lifted into the mother ship bomb bay.

During flight testing the XF-85 performed reasonably in the air, however, hooking back up to the mother ship proved to be extremely hazardous due to sever buffeting. During the XF-85's first free flight the canopy was shattered during the attempted in-flight hook-up to the trapeze on the mother ship resulting in the aircraft having to make an emergency landing on the dry lakebed at Muroc. During later flights an air cushion effect was detected when the mother ship and XF-85 attempted to hook-up. This was exacerbated by the complex structure of the trapeze, which was central to the Parasite fighter concept.

The XF-85 flight tests were conducted over Muroc Dry Lake Bed (now Edwards AFB), California. During one such flight, the aircraft's canopy shattered when it struck the trapeze apparatus, requiring the pilot to conduct an emergency landing. Other problems during testing included turbulence, which prevented the aircraft from being hooked up to the EB-29, resulting in un-planned landings on the Dry Lake Bed. USAF

A number of flights resulting in unsuccessful hook-ups in the air saw the small stubby fighter forced to land on the Lake Bed on its steel skid. In the end, enough was enough; the difficulties encountered in the program along with advances being made in the field of air to air refuelling led to the programs cancellation.

XF-85: 2 development parasite fighter aircraft ordered under an initial contract in October 1945 under the designation XP-85. The first free flight was conducted on 23 August 1948 under the designation XF-85.

XF-85
Engines: One Westinghouse J35 turbojet rated at 3,000-lb thrust
Length: 14-ft 1-in
Height: 8-ft 3-in
Wingspan: 21-ft 1-in
Weights: 4,550-lb
Maximum speed: 650-mph (design speed, not attained)
Combat speed: 581-mph
Combat ceiling: 46,750-ft
Maximum endurance: 1-hour 20-minutes
Armament: four x 0.5-in heavy machine guns
Crew: One

Glossary

AAA	Anti Aircraft Artillery
ADC	Air Defence Command
AFB	Air Force Base
AFFTC	Air Force Flight Test Centre
ANG	Air National Guard
ATC	Air Training Command
B	Bomber
DFRC	Dryden Flight Research Centre
DoD	Department of Defence
F	Fighter
FB	Fighter Bomber
FEG	Fighter Escort Group
FG	Fighter Group
FICON	Fighter Conveyor
FIG	Fighter Interception Group
FIS	Fighter Interception Squadron
FS	Fighter Squadron
GOR	General Operational Requirement
HSFS	High Speed Flight Station
HVAR	High Velocity Aircraft Rockets
Kg	Kilogram
Km	Kilometre
LABS	Low Altitude Bombing System
M	Metre
MAP	Military Assistance Program
MDAP	Mutual Defence Assistance Program
MPH	Miles per Hour
NACA	National Advisory Committee on Aeronautics
NASA	National Aeronautic and Space Administration
NATO	North Atlantic Treaty Organisation
NORAD	North American Air Defence
P	Pursuit
PF	Photographic Fighter
PLAAF	Peoples Liberation Army Air Force
SAC	Strategic Air Command
SFW	Strategic Fighter Wing
S/N	Serial Number
SR	Strategic Reconnaissance
SRW	Strategic Reconnaissance Wing
TAC	Tactical Air Command
TF	Trainer Fighter
TFW	Tactical Fighter Wing
US	United States
USAAF	United States Army Air Force
USAF	United States Air Force
USAFM	United States Air Force Museum
USN	United States Navy
XA	Experimental Attack
XF	Experimental Fighter
XP	Experimental Pursuit

Centurion Publishing

ISBN 13: 978-1-903630-31-0

www.ingramcontent.com/pod-product-compliance
Lightning Source LLC
Chambersburg PA
CBHW071311040426
42444CB00009B/1981